Musonius Rufus

Musonius Rufus

Lectures & Sayings

Revised Edition

Translated with an Introduction by
Cynthia King

Edited with a Preface by
William B. Irvine

CreateSpace

Published in 2011
by William B. Irvine
at www.CreateSpace.com

Copyright © 2010, 2011 by Cynthia King

All rights reserved. No part of this book may be reprinted or reproduced or utilized in any form or by any electronic, mechanical, or other means, now known or hereafter invented, including photocopying and recording, or in any information storage or retrieval system, without permission in writing from the publisher.

ISBN-13: 978-1456459666

To W.J.K.

quod non exspectes ex transverso fit

Contents

Editor's Preface	9
Translator's Introduction	13
Part One: The Lectures of Musonius	21
Part Two: The Sayings of Musonius	83
Appendix I: Musonius in Philostratus	93
Appendix II: Letter to Pankratides	95
Acknowledgments	99

Editor's Preface

Gaius Musonius Rufus (c. AD 30–100) was one of the four great Roman Stoic philosophers, the other three being Seneca, Epictetus, and Marcus Aurelius. Musonius had a considerable following while alive and after his death was admired by philosophers and theologians alike. Today, though, he is the least well known of the Roman Stoics. This is unfortunate, inasmuch as familiarity with the views of Musonius is essential if we are fully to understand Roman Stoicism. In particular, the insights of Musonius are indispensable if our goal is not so much to explore Stoicism as a philosophical theory as to discover what it means to be a practicing Stoic.

Stoicism, like many of the ancient schools of philosophy, can trace its intellectual lineage back to Socrates. Many of Socrates' pupils went on to start schools of their own. Thus, we find Plato founding the Academy, Euclides founding the Megarian school, and Antisthenes founding the Cynic school. The Cynics were the most ascetic of the post-Socratic philosophers; they were the ancient equivalent of what we today would call the homeless. They also had little tolerance for philosophical speculation regarding justice, beauty, or metaphysics; to the contrary, their goal was to determine how to live a good life and to help those they encountered live one.

Antisthenes had Diogenes of Sinope as a pupil, who had Crates as a pupil, who in turn had Zeno of Citium as a pupil. Zeno soon realized that Cynic asceticism did not agree with him. He also concluded that the Cynics were mistaken to have so thoroughly rejected philosophical speculation. He therefore left Crates to study under Polemo of the Academy and Stilpo of the Megarian school, and in around 300 BC, Zeno started his own school of philosophy. At first his pupils were called Zenonians, but because they were in the habit of meeting in the Stoa Poikile, a colonnade decorated with murals, they became known as the Stoics. After Zeno's death, Cleanthes and then Chrysippus inherited leadership of the Stoic school. In 140 BC, Panaetius traveled to Rome and took Stoicism with him, thus giving rise to the Roman variant of the philosophy.

As practiced by the Greeks, Stoicism had three components: logic, physics, and ethics. The Stoics' interest in logic was a consequence of their belief that man is by nature a rational animal: by studying logic the Stoics sought to make the best use of their reasoning ability. The Stoics also had another, more pragmatic reason to study logic: students attended their schools in part so they could develop their persuasive abilities. Stoic physics was concerned not only with explaining the nature of the world around them but with explaining their relationship to the gods. And finally, Stoic ethics was not ethics in the modern sense of the word—it was not, that is, concerned with questions of moral right and wrong. It was instead concerned with what one must do to have a good life.

According to the Stoics, the best way to have a good life is to pursue virtue, and the best way to pursue virtue is to fulfill the function for which the gods created us: what we should seek to do, the Stoics said, is "live in accordance with nature." Since the gods gave us reasoning ability—and in doing so set us apart from other animals—the Stoics concluded that if we want to have a good life, we need to behave in a rational manner, and this in turn means that we need to learn how to control our emotions. Indeed, according to the Stoics, a person whose emotions are out of control—who is given to fits of anger, fear, envy, lust, or despair—is little better than a beast. Such a person is unlikely to have a good life.

The Stoics' apparent rejection of emotions has made a great impression on modern minds. Ask someone to characterize the Stoics, and he is likely to resort to adjectives such as *impassive, aloof,* or even *wooden.* This perception, however, is very much mistaken. It is true that some ancient sources portrayed the Greek Stoics as seeking to overcome all emotion. It is also true that the idealized sage described by the Stoic philosophers seems to have been devoid of emotion. What we need to keep in mind, though, is that the Stoic philosophers themselves were not emotionless beings. For one thing, they do not appear to have been immune to negative emotions, such as anger, fear, envy, grief, and anxiety, although they do appear to have been significantly less susceptible to these emotions than most people are. Furthermore, they seem to have welcomed the experience of positive emotions: indeed, they were apparently notable for their cheerfulness. Thus, the phrase "joyful Stoic" is not the oxymoron many would take it to be.

The Greek Stoics, as we have seen, studied logic, physics, and ethics; the Roman Stoics, though, were almost exclusively interested in ethics. They concerned themselves with what we should do if we wish to have a good life and consequently thought long and hard about the negative emotions that disrupt our tranquility in everyday living. As a result, their writings are full of advice on how to prevent ourselves from experiencing negative emotions and on how, when our attempts at prevention fail, we can extinguish these emotions. Some of the advice is philosophical: by choosing the right values, they argue, we can dramatically improve our chances of attaining tranquility. Most of the advice, though, is psychological in nature. Thus, we find Seneca explaining at length how to avoid getting upset when someone insults us and how to overcome the grief we might experience on the death of a relative.

It is for this reason that, in the lectures of Musonius, we find little in the way of physics and logic; instead we find him dispensing advice on how to have a good life. Among the questions he considers: Should kings study philosophy? Briefly, yes (Lecture 8). Should women study philosophy? Again, yes (Lectures 3 and 4)—an answer, by the way, that has endeared Musonius to modern feminists. Is exile an evil? Surprisingly, no (Lecture 9). Should men grow beards? Probably (Lecture 21). And what is the best occupation for a philosopher? Farming (Lecture 11).

The Stoics, as we have seen, abandoned the rigorous asceticism of the Cynics. The Stoics themselves differed, though, in the extent to which they thought we should enjoy life. Musonius appears to have been relatively austere. He counsels against sex outside of marriage (Lecture 12); he is, however, an advocate of marriage (Lectures 13 and 14). He counsels us to eat and live simply (Lectures 18–20). He also thinks that, besides not allowing ourselves to become slaves to comfort, we should go out of our way to cause ourselves needless discomfort (Lectures 6 and 19). We should, for example, make a point of underdressing for cold weather, going shoeless, or sleeping on a hard bed. The goal in doing this is not to inflict pain on ourselves but, paradoxically, to increase our enjoyment of life.

According to Musonius, philosophy, done properly, should affect us personally and profoundly. Indeed, Musonius measured the success of a philosophy lecture not by how much applause it generated but by whether it reduced its audience to silence (Sayings 48 and 49). The silence in question would be the result of the lecture revealing to the members of the audience their shortcomings as human beings. And this, according to Musonius, should be one of the primary objectives of philosophy: to reveal to us our shortcomings so we can overcome them and thereby live a good life.

Musonius' lectures, because they are long on practical advice and short on theory, are quite accessible. They also give us insight into what it meant, in ancient Rome, to be a practicing Stoic. And for those whose interests are cultural rather than philosophical, they provide us with a window into daily life in first-century Rome.

Musonius' reputation outlived him. Thus, more than a century after Musonius' death, philosopher and theologian Origen, in discussing individuals who could be held up as examples of living "the best life," mentions two philosophers, Socrates and Musonius. By the end of the twentieth century, though, Musonius had fallen into obscurity. While the works of the other Roman Stoics could be obtained in most libraries and bookstores, the works of Musonius were surprisingly difficult to obtain. There was only one translation into English of his works—made by Cora Lutz in 1947—and where I live, only one tattered copy of this translation was available through inter-library loan. The translation that follows is an attempt to remedy this situation and help return Musonius to his rightful place in the Stoic pantheon.

WILLIAM B. IRVINE

Translator's Introduction

The Stoic philosopher Gaius Musonius Rufus[1] was by birth a Roman *eques* ("knight," an aristocratic ranking only below senators) who was born before AD 30 and died before 101/2. He was exiled under Nero, returning under Galba, and was exiled again under Vespasian, returning under Titus. Musonius taught the Stoic philosopher Epictetus, who refers to his master as Rufus in his own writings. Musonius makes his first appearance in history in AD 62 in the *Annals* of Tacitus (c. AD 55–117), who says he is of Etruscan origin, and lists him as one of the philosophical friends of Rubellius Plautus (14.59.1). Plautus, as the son of Tiberius' granddaughter, was a threat to Nero, who exiled him to Asia Minor, and subsequently had him murdered. Musonius apparently accompanied Plautus in his exile; Musonius' exile in AD 65 is noted in *Annals* 15.71.4.

Musonius appears again as a peace negotiator in Tacitus' description, in the *Histories*, of the confused events of AD 69. Following the ouster and death of Nero, a civil war took place, and there was a struggle for power among Galba, Otto, Vitellius, and Vespasian (3.81.1):

> A knight named Musonius Rufus had attached himself to the envoys. He was a student of philosophy and an enthusiastic advocate of Stoicism. He mingled with the companies, offering the armed soldiers advice and discoursing on the advantages of peace and the perils of war. This amused many of them and bored still more. Some, indeed, wanted to knock and trample him down, but the advice of the more sober spirits and the threats of others persuaded him to cut short his ill-timed lecture.[2]

After Vespasian became emperor (and while Domitian was handling affairs in Rome), Musonius makes his final appearance in the *Histories* (4.10, 4.40): in AD 70, he secured the conviction of the philosopher Publius Egnatius Celer, who had betrayed Barea Soranus, a friend of Rubellius Plautus.[3] The evidence for Musonius' second exile under

---

[1] The typical name for a Roman man has three parts: *praenomen* or first name, *nomen* or family name—what we would call our last name, and *cognomen*, another family name.

[2] W. H. Fyfe's translation of Tacitus' *Histories*, as revised by D. S. Levene (Oxford World Classics, 1997) p. 166.

[3] D. S. Levene notes in his comment on *Histories* 3.81.8 (n. 2, above, p. 276) that Musonius must have been a senator to conduct this prosecution, and he says that Tacitus may be referring to Musonius as a knight loosely, and mean only that he was of equestrian

Vespasian and return under Titus comes from later sources. His death can be dated by reference to Pliny the Younger (c. AD 61–112), who speaks of Musonius in the past tense when discussing Musonius' son-in-law, the Greek philosopher Artemidorus, in a letter dated about AD 101 (3.11.5).

Most of the remains of Musonius—I am going to call them Lectures (1–21) and Sayings (22–53), as I will explain below—are preserved in a fifth-century *Anthology* by Stobaeus (John of Stobi). Stobaeus' work is not completely preserved, but we know its overall layout from Photius, a ninth-century church figure who included it in his mammoth review of books; this work has been given the title of *Bibliotheca*. Each section of Photius is called a "codex"; codex 167 contains his account of Stobaeus. He tells us that Stobaeus' work was entitled *Extracts, Sayings, Admonitions*, and that it consisted of four books in two volumes. The first book dealt with natural sciences, the second with logic and ethics, and the third and fourth with ethics and politics. The first and second books are not well-preserved in the manuscript tradition. No Musonius material appears in Book 1. Five lectures and one saying come from Book 2, but most of the Musonius material comes from Books 3 and 4.

Stobaeus organized the selections in his books into chapters and gave these chapters titles, some of which are very long. Photius lists the titles, and they usually match with the titles as they appear in the manuscripts. Where the manuscripts are faulty, Photius enables us to see what is missing. In Book 4 Stobaeus divided some chapters into parts. For example, Musonius' Lecture 14 comes from Stobaeus 4.22a.20. It comes, that is, from Excerpt 20 ("By Musonius—from the lecture on whether marriage gets in the way of studying philosophy") of Part A ("that marriage is the best thing") of Chapter 22 ("about marriage") of Book 4.

Musonius apparently lectured in Greek. His ideas were preserved by others, especially by a certain Lucius whose name appears in connection with Lecture 5. Musonius apparently wrote nothing himself.

---

family. Soranus had been Celer's pupil; both were Stoics. Demetrius of Corinth, a Cynic philosopher who appears in Seneca's writings in a favorable light, defended Celer and thus earned Tacitus' scorn. See Michael Trapp, "Cynics," in *Greek and Roman Philosophy 100 BC–200 AD*, Vol I, edited by Richard Sorabji and Robert W. Sharples (*Bulletin of the Institute of Classical Studies* Supplement 94, 2007) pp. 201–3.

Lucius' model is Xenophon, who preserved "recollections" of Socrates.[4] Arrian performed a similar function for Epictetus.[5]

The standard publication of Musonius is *C. Musonii Rufi Reliquiae*, edited by O. Hense (Leipzig, 1905). The standard publication of Stobaeus is *Ioannis Stobaei Anthologii libri duo priores I–II*, edited by C. Wachsmuth (Berlin, 1884), and *Ioannis Stobaei Anthologii libri duo posteriores III–V*, edited by O. Hense (Berlin, 1894–1923, repr. 1958). Hense made some minor changes in the text of the Musonius extracts in his Stobaeus IV. The standard publication of Photius is in the Budé Byzantine series with Greek text and French translation. The Stobaeus section is in Photius, *Bibliothèque*, Tome II ("codices" 84–185), edited and translated by René Henry (Paris, 1960) pp. 149–59.

The Musonius remains are divided as follows:

- 21 longer selections (Lectures), in Stobaeus—usually headed *Mousoniou ek tou*, "Of Musonius, from the Lecture on [so and so]";
- 14 Sayings, also in Stobaeus—usually headed *Mousoniou*, "Of Musonius";
- 5 Sayings, in Stobaeus—"Of Rufus, from Epictetus, On Friendship";
- 6 Sayings, from Epictetus' *Discourses* (Arrian);[6]
- 2 Sayings, from Plutarch's *Moralia*;[7]
- 4 Sayings, from Aulus Gellius (in Latin);[8]
- 1 saying, from Aelius Aristides.[9]

---

[4] The term in Greek for this work of Xenophon is *Apomnemoneumata* ("Recollections") of Socrates. In the Renaissance it was given the Latin title, *Memorabilia* ("things worth remembering").

[5] Michael B. Trapp, *Philosophy in the Roman Empire: Ethics, Politics and Society* (Ashgate, 2007) consistently refers to Epictetus as "Arrian's Epictetus." Perhaps we should refer to Musonius as "Lucius' Musonius."

[6] Arrian (c. AD 86–160), a Greek who became a Roman senator and consul, wrote histories and philosophy; his model was Xenophon.

[7] Plutarch of Chaeronea (before AD 50–c.120), a Greek who held offices under Rome, was a philosopher and biographer. The *Moralia* (moral things) is a catch-all title for this collection of a vast amount of topics.

[8] Aulus Gellius (born c. AD 125–8) was author of *Attic Nights*, a collection of short chapters in Latin on a variety of topics such as philosophy, history, law, and literature, based on his extensive reading. He decided to make this compilation during long winter nights in Attica.

[9] Aelius Aristides (AD 117–after 181), a Greek from Asia Minor, was a sophist and author of public and private speeches, essays, prose hymns, and *Sacred Discourses* (what the healing god Asclepius told him in dreams).

Scholarly references to Musonius are to Hense's text with page numbers; this is awkward for a translation, and I have divided the lectures into numbered paragraphs.

The only complete English translation of Musonius, printing Hense's 1905 text with some minor changes, is Cora Lutz, "Musonius Rufus 'the Roman Socrates'," *Yale Classical Studies* 10 (1947): pp. 32–147, Greek text and English translation; pp. 3–31, thorough introduction. Lutz did not use vols. 4 and 5 of the Hense Stobaeus for the Musonius material which comes from Stobaeus IV. I also use Hense's Musonius text, but I check his Stobaeus for the excerpts from Book IV.[10] A very useful French translation with introduction and notes is Amand Jagu, *Musonius Rufus, Entretiens et Fragments, Introduction, Traduction et Commentaire*, in *Studien und Materialien zur Geschichte der Philosophie, Kleine Reihe*, Band I (Olms, 1979). There is no commentary on the Greek text itself.

What should the "remains" of Musonius be called? Hense's edition called them just that, *reliquiae*, "remains" (introduction, commentary, and critical apparatus in scholarly editions of classical texts are in Latin).[11] In connection with her discussion of the longer selections, Lutz uses the following terms: "discourses," "conversations" (*entretiens* in French), "treatises," and "diatribes."[12] But these longer selections

---

[10] For Sayings 36–37, which come from Plutarch's *Moralia*, I have also consulted the Loeb edition for Vol. VI (W. C. Helmbold, 1939, repr. 1970) and Vol. X (H. N. Fowler, 1936, repr. 1969).

For the material from Epictetus, I follow W. A. Oldfather's Loeb edition for Sayings 43–45 (Vol. I, Arrian's Discourses of Epictetus I–II, 1925, repr. 1989) and for Sayings 38–42, 46–48 (*Discourses* III–IV and Fragments, 1928, repr. 1985). I add the next sentence from Epictetus in Saying 45 (*Discourses* 1.9.32) to what Hense and Lutz use in order to try to clarify the meaning of Musonius' remark. In Saying 48, I add the next two sections in which Epictetus is speaking, again to clarify Musonius' point (*Discourses* 3.23.30–32). One should also note the 1916 translation of Epictetus by P. E. Matheson used in *The Stoic and Epicurean Philosophers*, edited by Whitney J. Oates (Modern Library, 1940).

For the material from Aulus Gellius' *Attic Nights*, I have consulted J. C. Rolfe's Loeb edition of 1927 and use Gellius' section headings for Sayings 49–51. Saying 49 comes from Vol. I (rev. and repr. 1946, repr. 1970). Saying 50 comes from Vol. II (repr. 1968). Sayings 51–52 come from Vol. III (rev. and repr. 1952, repr. 1967); I add more context to Saying 52 than Hense and Lutz provide.

[11] The scholarly edition previous to Hense uses *reliquiae* ("remains") and *apophthegmata* ("sayings") in its title: I. V. Peerlkamp, *C. Musonii Rufi Philosophi Stoici Reliquiae et Apophthegmata* (Haarlem, 1822).

[12] Lutz, pp. 6–7, nn. 12–13. The term "diatribe" in antiquity was used as the title for an account, written by someone else, of a philosopher's "lectures" and would have been a good label except that its modern meaning connotes a harangue. See Trapp, "Cynics," pp. 195–8 (n. 3 above).

are usually interpreted as the lecture notes of Lucius recording Musonius' lectures, and so I have chosen to call them "Lectures." Lutz calls the second group "short apothegms," "precepts," "anecdotes," "fragments," and "aphorisms."[13] I am calling them "Sayings."

Evidence for the existence of a collection of Musonius' lectures comes from a third-century papyrus which contains Musonius' Lecture 15a, and shows not only that Stobaeus did not quote all of this lecture, but that he adjusted the beginning of the excerpt. There are examples of works of other authors that Stobaeus excerpts and alters so that the excerpts become complete units.[14] J. Enoch Powell's initial publication of this papyrus shows that it comes from an "elegantly written" roll and has two columns of writing, "complete at top and bottom." Column i is badly damaged, but Powell was able to read enough of column ii to provide a translation of it from line 4 to its end at line 50.[15] The next year, following advice from M. P. Charlesworth, he identified the papyrus as containing what Stobaeus preserved in his fifth-century anthology as one of two excerpts from a lecture by Musonius on raising all children who are born (4.24a.15; 15a in Hense's Musonius edition) and published the full text using the manuscript tradition for Stobaeus to fill in the gaps in the papyrus.[16] Stobaeus started this excerpt three-fourths of the way through the second line of column i of the papyrus as it is preserved. Most of line 1 is missing, and it is not clear whether this was the actual beginning of the lecture. Not only does the papyrus contain all of 15a (column i, lines 2–51; column ii, lines 1–32), but it goes beyond it in column ii, lines 33–50. There are twenty to twenty-four letters in a line.

The provocative British historian, G. E. M. de Ste. Croix mentions Musonius Rufus favorably with regard to his views on women.[17] Martha Nussbaum is less complimentary and characterizes Musonius'

---

[13] Lutz, p. 8.

[14] David A. Campbell, "Stobaeus and Early Greek Lyric Poetry," in *Greek Poetry and Philosophy: Studies in Honour of Leonard Woodbury*, edited by Douglas E. Gerber (Scholars Press, 1984) p. 56, n. 9.

[15] *The Rendel Harris Papyri* (Cambridge, 1936) pp. 1–5, pl. 1, lower right (col. ii, lines 25–50). Dr. James Rendel Harris was Curator of Manuscripts at the Rylands Library in Manchester; he bought a collection of papyri in Egypt in 1922–23 (preface, p. v).

[16] "Musonius Rufus: *Ei panta ta ginomena tekna threpteon*," *Archiv für Papyrusforschung* 12 (1937): 175–8. M. P. Charlesworth had included Musonius in his *Five Men: Character Studies from the Roman Empire*, Martin Classical Studies VI (1936): The Philosopher, pp. 31–62.

[17] *The Class Struggle in the Ancient Greek World from the Archaic Age to the Arab Conquests* (Cornell, 1981) p. 110, n. 28 (p. 557).

feminism as "incomplete."[18] Simon Goldhill also discusses Musonius' views on women, especially the bold idea in Lecture 4 that a woman should be manly—should, that is, exhibit *andreia* ("manliness, courage").[19] Musonius has also benefited from the relatively recent and mainly British attention to "Greek culture and society between AD 50 and 250, the period known as the 'second sophistic'."[20] Tim Whitmarsh, in his introduction to a general study of the period, gives reasons for this interest:

> The Greek literary culture of the first three centuries of this era is no longer viewed as an embarrassing epilogue. It is not just that this is the period of Greek history from which we have the most material . . . . Aesthetic values have changed: the Romantic obsession with "originality" and "inspiration" has been challenged by newer emphases on "creative imitation," and indeed (under the influence of postmodernism) the reception, replication, and intertextual refashioning of earlier literary works. Political priorities have also shifted: that Greeks of that period were under Roman occupation is now more likely to inspire sympathetic analyses of colonial politics than dismissive sniffs at a weak and decadent culture. Finally, with all its abundant and frequently exuberant prose literature, the Greek world of the early empire is a wonderful source for those inspired by newer intellectual methodologies, predominantly social and cultural anthropology, gender studies, cultural studies, and the history of sexuality.[21]

In a more detailed examination of this period, Whitmarsh includes a study of Musonius as something of a disaffected exile; he also looks at Musonius' views on women.[22]

---

[18] See "The Incomplete Feminism of Musonius Rufus, Platonist, Stoic, and Roman" in *The Sleep of Reason: Erotic Experience and Sexual Ethics in Ancient Greece and Rome*, edited by Martha C. Nussbaum and Juha Sihvola (Chicago, 2002) pp. 283–326. See also her earlier essay, "Musonius Rufus: Enemy of Double Standards for Men and Women?" in *Double Standards in the Ancient and Medieval Worlds*, edited by Karla Pollmann, Gottinger Forum für Altertumswissenschaft, Beihefte 1 (Göttingen, 2000) pp. 221–46.

[19] *Foucault's Virginity: Ancient Erotic Fiction and the History of Sexuality* (Cambridge, 1995) pp. 132–43.

[20] S. C. R. Swain, *Hellenism and Empire: Language, Classicism, and Power in the Greek World, AD 50–250* (Oxford, 1996) p. 1.

[21] *The Second Sophistic* (*Greece and Rome: New Surveys in the Classics* no. 35; Oxford, 2005) p. 1.

[22] *Greek Literature and the Roman Empire: The Politics of Imitation* (Oxford, 2001) Chapter 3: "Rome Uncivilized: Exile and the Kingdom," pp. 133–80, particularly pp. 141–55 ("Musonius Rufus, the 'Roman' 'Socrates' "); views on women, pp. 112–3.

It is important for us to understand the context in which the Musonius extracts survived and the fragility of the transmission of his ideas. The 21 fairly long extracts in Stobaeus' *Anthology* are essentially a student's lecture notes. But Stobaeus never seems to give the whole of a lecture (this is confirmed for Lecture 15 to which there is independent witness from the papyrus which survived by chance), and he breaks up several lectures to fit into the different categories which he wishes to illustrate. We know this because he almost always gives the title of the lecture from which he is taking the excerpt.

Musonius has become popular in recent years for his insistence that both women and men should be educated, for his rejection of a double standard (although feminists debate his feminism), and for his resistance to autocracy (speaking truth to power). He is an "outsider insider," a Roman who expressed his ideas in Greek, and he looms large in the scholarly discussion of what it meant to be Greek under the Roman Empire. And of course, his philosophical ideas on ethics have always been of interest. He reminds me most of Tacitus' insistence, regarding his father-in-law Agricola, that one can be a great man even under a bad ruler.[23] Musonius shows us how, under such circumstances, one can be a *good* man.

C. K.

---

[23] *Agricola* 42: *posse etiam sub malis principibus magnos viros esse* ("great men can exist even under bad rulers").

Part One

The Lectures of Musonius

1. By Musonius, from the lecture showing that one does not need to use many arguments to prove one point

(1) Once when there was a discussion about the arguments which young people should hear from philosophers in order to master what they are learning, Musonius said that rather than seeking many proofs on each subject, we should seek practical and clear ones. It is not the doctor who brings many drugs to sick people who deserves praise, he said, but rather the one who helps them in a noteworthy manner with the few drugs which he prescribes. The philosopher who teaches his listeners with many proofs is not to be praised either, but rather the one who guides them to where he wants them with a few. And the more intelligent the listener is, the fewer proofs that listener will need and the more quickly he will agree to the discussion's main point, at least if it is sound. The person who requires a detailed argument even where the evidence is clear or who wants things which could be proved by few arguments to be demonstrated to him in many is completely absurd and dull.

(2) It is a reasonable assumption that the gods need no argument to prove anything, because nothing is unclear or uncertain to them. One needs arguments to prove only those things that are unclear or uncertain. Things that are neither clear nor knowable in and of themselves people must seek to discover from clear and plain things, since this is argument's task. An example is the proposition that pleasure is not a good thing. This does not seem to be self-evident, since pleasure in fact attracts us as if it were a good. But if we take the well-known premise that every good is desirable and if we add to this the second well-known premise that some pleasures are not desirable, we show that pleasure is not a good—we show the unfamiliar through the familiar. Again, the proposition that pain is not an evil does not seem in and of itself convincing: the opposite of this, that pain is an evil, seems more plausible. But when the clear premise is established, that every evil is to be avoided, and when an even clearer premise is added to it, that many pains are not to be avoided, the conclusion is that pain is not an evil.

(3) This is the proper form of argumentation. But since some people are sharper and others are duller, and since some have been raised with better values and others with worse, the ones who have an

---

[24] Stobaeus 2.31.125. Chapter 31: on training and education.

inferior character or nature would need more arguments and more hard work so that they accept these teachings and are shaped by them, just as I think that unfit bodies also require much more attention if they are going to get well.

(4) Young people who are more intelligent and better educated would accept correct reasoning more easily, quickly, and with fewer arguments, and would act in accordance with this reasoning. That this is the case, we could easily learn if we would think of a boy or young man raised amid every luxury, made womanish in body, and weakened in spirit by habits leading to softness—and who has a dull and stupid nature to boot. Compare this young man with another one brought up in a somewhat Spartan manner, not accustomed to live in luxury, but trained to endure and inclined to listen to correct reasoning. If we then were to make these two young men listen to a philosopher speaking about death, pain, poverty, and such things—that they are not evil—and again in turn about life, pleasure, wealth, and things similar to these—that they are not good—will both young men accept the conclusions in the same way and would each one be equally persuaded by them? Certainly not.

(5) The first young man—the duller one—barely and slowly pried loose, as it were, by a thousand words, perhaps would agree. The other young man, though, will quickly and readily accept the conclusions as natural and suitable for himself without needing many arguments or more study. Is not this second young man like the Spartan boy who asked Cleanthes the philosopher if pain was not a good? That boy seems to have been so naturally good and to have been trained so well towards virtue that he considered pain to be closer to the nature of a good than of an evil. He asked if pain happened to be a good, since the argument that it was not an evil was understood already by him. In admiration for the boy, Cleanthes quoted a verse from the *Odyssey* to him:

You are of good blood, dear child, because of the kind of words you say.[25]

How, then, could such a boy not easily be persuaded to fear neither poverty nor death nor any other of the things which seem dreadful, and again not to seek wealth or life or pleasure?

(6) Returning to the beginning of my discussion, I say that the teacher of philosophy should not seek to go through an abundance of

---

[25] Homer, *Odyssey*, 4.611.

words and arguments for those who are learning, but should instead speak appropriately about each subject and reach the understanding of his listener and say things which he knows are persuasive and not easily overturned.[26] Most of all he should present himself both as one speaking about the most useful things and as one doing things in agreement with what he says, and in this way he should deal with his listeners. The student should pay close attention to the things which are said and watch out that he does not inadvertently accept some falsehood. But by Zeus, he must seek to hear not many proofs of true things, but rather plain ones, and in his life he must follow whatever lessons he is persuaded are true. Only by exhibiting actions in harmony with the sound words which he has received will anyone be helped by philosophy.

---

[26] There may be a lacuna or gap in the text here.

2. By Musonius[27]

(1) Each and every one of us, he said, is disposed by nature to live without error and honorably. Indeed, this is convincingly demonstrated by the fact that law-givers both prescribe what one must do and proscribe what one must not do, and they allow no one who disobeys or does wrong to escape punishment: not a young person, not an old man, not a strong man, not a weak one—no one at all. And yet, if the whole concept of virtue were not innate and if nothing of it were shared with us by nature, then just as no one is expected to be error-free in activities connected with other skills if he has not learned that skill, so it would not be appropriate for someone who has not learned virtue to be expected to be error-free in activities connected with living, since virtue alone keeps us from making errors in living.

(2) As it is, no one expects anyone other than the doctor to be error-free in the care of the sick, anyone other than the musician to be error-free in the use of the lyre, and anyone other than the helmsman to be error-free in the use of steering-oars. But in connection with life, people no longer expect only the philosopher, who alone seems to make a study of virtue, to be error-free; rather, they expect all people likewise to be, even those who have not made any study of virtue. Clearly, there is no other reason for this attitude than the innate human proclivity for virtue. Indeed, that we all say about ourselves that we have virtue and are good also clearly demonstrates that we share in virtue by nature.

(3) No ordinary person will admit to being witless if asked whether he happens to be witless or wise; nor will he, if asked whether he happens to be unjust or just, say that he is unjust. Likewise if someone asks him whether he is self-controlled or self-indulgent, he answers[28] upon being questioned that he is self-controlled. To sum up, if someone asks him whether he is good or bad, he would say that he is good, even though he could not say either who his teacher of proper living was or what study or training in virtue he happened to have undertaken.

(4) What does this prove, other than that there is an inborn capacity in the human being's soul for proper living and that the seed

---

[27] Stobaeus 2.9.8. Chapter 9: that no one errs willingly. Stobaeus does not provide a title for this excerpt.

[28] There is a crux or problem in the text here; I omit the problematic word.

of virtue exists in each one of us? Because it is entirely fitting for us to be good, some of us deceive ourselves into thinking that we are indeed good, and others of us are ashamed to admit that we are not. A person who has not studied letters, music, or sports does not say that he knows them. Nor does he pretend to possess these skills if he is unable to name also the teacher to whom he went. So why, by the gods, do we all declare that we have virtue? A human being has no claim by nature to any of those other skills, and no one comes into life with a natural ability for them.[29]

---

[29] There may be a lacuna in the text here.

3. By Musonius, from the lecture showing that women also should study philosophy[30]

(1) When someone asked him if women also should study philosophy, he began to teach, along lines like the following, how they should do it. For one thing, he said, women have received from the gods the same reasoning power as men—the power which we employ with each other and according to which we consider whether each action is good or bad, and honorable or shameful. Likewise the female has also the same senses as the male: seeing, hearing, ability to smell, and the rest. Likewise, too, each has the same parts of the body, and neither one has more than the other. In addition, a desire for virtue and an affinity for it belong by nature not only to men but also to women: no less than men are they disposed by nature to be pleased by noble and just deeds and to censure things opposite these.

(2) Since this is so, why would it be appropriate for men but not women to seek to live honorably and consider how to do so, which is what studying philosophy is? Is it appropriate for men to be good, but not women? Let us also consider, one by one, each of the attributes which are appropriate for a woman who would be good, for it will be apparent that each one of these would come to her most easily from philosophy.

(3) To begin with, a woman must be able to manage an estate, to keep account of things beneficial to it, and to take charge of the household staff. I say that these things would be most characteristic of the woman who pursues philosophy, since each of these is a part of life, and knowledge concerning life is what philosophy is. Furthermore, as Socrates, quoting a verse from the *Odyssey*, used to say, the philosopher has as his goal investigating

What evil and good has been done in your halls.[31]

But a woman must also be self-controlled: she must be free from sexual improprieties and must exercise self-control over other pleasures; she must not be a slave to desires; she must not be quarrelsome, extravagant, or vain. These are the characteristics of the self-controlled

---

[30] Stobaeus 2.31.126. Chapter 31: on training and education.

[31] Homer, *Odyssey*, 4.392.

woman, as are the following: controlling anger, not being overcome by grief, and being stronger than every emotion.

(4) Philosophic study transmits these things: it seems to me that a person who has studied and practiced them would exhibit the most beautiful character, whether man or woman. What then? These things are so. Would not a woman who studies philosophy be just? Would she not be a blameless partner in life, a good co-worker and like-minded one, a careful guardian of husband and children, entirely free from the love of gain or grasping for too much? And who, more than a female philosopher (and it is entirely necessary for her to think thus, if she were really a philosopher) would think it worse to do wrong (insofar as it is more shameful) than to be wronged? Likewise, who, more than a female philosopher, would think that suffering loss is better than taking more than one's share? And in addition, who, more than she, would love her children more than life? What woman would be more just than such a woman as this?

(5) Now surely it is appropriate for an educated woman to be braver than an uneducated woman and for a woman trained in philosophy to be braver than one untrained in it. Furthermore, it is appropriate for her not to submit to anything shameful because she fears death or is afraid of pain. It is also appropriate for her not to bow down to anyone, be he well-born, powerful, wealthy, or even, by Zeus, a tyrant. It stands her in good stead to have learned to think nobly and to consider death not an evil and life not a good, and at the same time it stands her in good stead not to turn pain aside and not to pursue lack of pain above all. Therefore it is likely that this woman would be both self-motivated and persevering, the kind of woman to nurse at her own breast the children whom she brings forth, to serve her husband with her own hands, and to do without hesitation tasks which some consider appropriate for slaves.

(6) Would not a woman like this be a great advantage for the man who has married her, a source of honor for those related to her by birth, and a good example for the women who know her? But, by Zeus, some say that women who associate with philosophers are generally headstrong and brash, when they abandon their house-keeping and go around in public with men and practice arguments, act like sophists, and analyze syllogisms. These women, they say, should be sitting at home spinning wool. There is no way that I would expect women who pursue philosophy—or even men, for that matter—to cast aside their appropriate tasks and concern themselves with words

only, but I say that they should pursue the discussions they undertake for the sake of actions.

(7) Just as there is no use in medical study unless it leads to the health of the human body, so there is no use to a philosophical doctrine unless it leads to the virtue of the human soul. Above all, we must examine the doctrine which we deem is right for women who study philosophy to follow. Could following the doctrine which declares modesty to be the greatest good make women brash? Could following the doctrine which counsels the most restraint train them to live recklessly? Could following the doctrine which demonstrates that self-indulgence is the most terrible evil not teach them to exercise self-control? And could following the doctrine which presents managing one's estate as a virtue not lead them to be better managers? The doctrine of the philosophers encourages a woman to be happy and to rely on herself.

4. By Musonius, from the lecture on whether daughters should get the same education as sons[32]

(1) One time in a discussion on whether sons and daughters should get the same education, he said that those who train horses and dogs deal with males no differently from females. Female dogs are trained to hunt in the same way as males. And if one wants female horses to perform well the tasks of horses, they should not be trained differently than the males. In the case of humans, will it really be necessary for males and not females to have something special in their education and upbringing? As if it were not necessary for both a man and a woman alike to have the same virtues, or as if it were possible to achieve the same virtues not through the same lessons, but through different ones!

(2) It is obvious that there is not one type of virtue for a man and another for a woman. To begin with, a man must have good sense, and so must a woman. What, after all, would be the usefulness of a foolish man or woman? Both men and women must live in accordance with justice. A man would not be a good citizen if he is unjust, and a woman would not manage her household well, if she does not do it with justice. But if she is unjust, she will act unjustly towards her husband himself, as they say Eriphyle did.[33] Furthermore, it is as right for a woman to be self-controlled as it is for a man. The laws punish equally a man who seduces and the woman who is seduced. Overeating, drinking too much, and other vices like these, which are acts of self-indulgence and which greatly shame those who are subject to them, show plainly that self-control is most essential for every human being, both female and male: through self-control alone and in no other way do we escape self-indulgence.

(3) Someone might say that courage is an appropriate characteristic for men only, but this is not so. It is also necessary for a woman—at least for a most noble one—to be courageous and free from cowardice so that she is overcome neither by pain nor by fear. How, after all, can she have self-control if someone, by either causing fear or applying

---

[32] Stobaeus 2.31.123. Chapter 31: on training and education.

[33] Eriphyle was bribed by Polynices (see Lecture 9.8) with Harmonia's necklace to force her husband, the seer Amphiaraus, to join the Seven Against Thebes (cf. Aeschylus' play). Amphiaraus knew that the expedition would fail and he would die. Their son Alcmaeon avenged his death by killing his mother.

pain, can force her to submit to something shameful? Indeed women must also be ready to put up a fight, unless, by Zeus, they don't mind appearing inferior to hens and other female birds, which fight with animals much bigger than they are on behalf of their chicks. How, then, could women not need courage? The tribe of Amazons, when they overthrew many peoples with weapons, showed that women can participate in armed conflict. So if some women lack courage, it is from lack of practice rather than from courage not being an innate quality.[34]

(4) As far as the virtues of a man and a woman are concerned, it is entirely appropriate for both men and women to have the same upbringing and education. Indeed, for every animal and plant, proper care ought to produce the virtue appropriate for it. If a man and a woman had to be able to play the flute equally well, and if they each had to do this to earn their living, we would teach them both alike the art of flute-playing, as we would do with the cithara, if each of them had to learn to play it. If men and women must be equally good in the virtue appropriate for a human—must, that is, be wise and self-controlled, and share in courage and justice—will we not educate both alike, and teach both the same way the art by which a human would become good? We must do just that!

(5) Perhaps someone says: "What? Do you advise men to learn spinning along with women and women to pursue gymnastics along with men?!" I am not advising this, but I do say that since among humans the nature of males is stronger and of females is weaker, the most suitable tasks must be assigned to each nature, with the heavier ones being given to the stronger and the lighter ones being given to the weaker. As a result, spinning would be more suitable for women than for men, just as being indoors is, and gymnastics would be more suitable for men than for women, just as being outdoors is. But sometimes, when a health condition or circumstances require it, or when opportunity allows it, some men could reasonably undertake some of the lighter tasks and those which seem to be suited for women, and women in turn could perform some of the harder ones and those which seem to be more appropriate for men.

(6) All human affairs have a common basis and are therefore common to both men and women, and nothing has been exclusively reserved for either. Some things are more suited to one nature and some

---

[34] There is a lacuna or gap in the text between the end of this paragraph and the beginning of the next.

to the other; for this reason some things are called men's, others women's. If we say that virtues are no more appropriate for one group than the other, then it is correct to say that things pertaining to virtue are equally appropriate to each nature. Therefore, it is with good reason that I think both female and male must be trained in the same way in things pertaining to virtue.

(7) We must start by teaching infants that this thing is good and that thing is bad,[35] that this thing is helpful and that thing is harmful, and that this thing must be done and that thing must not be done. As a result of this teaching, a like understanding arises in the girls and boys who master the lesson, and nothing is different for either group. Then we must instill in them shame towards everything base. When understanding and shame exist, both man and woman will obviously be self-controlled. And the person educated correctly, whoever it be, whether male or female, must become accustomed to endure toil, to not fear death, and to not become dejected in the face of any misfortune. By doing these things, a person would become courageous. Earlier I showed that women also should possess courage. Surely to shun excess, to honor equality, to want to do good, and for a person, being human, to not want to harm human beings—this is the most honorable lesson and it makes just people out of those who learn it.

(8) Why does learning these things befit a man more than a woman? By Zeus, if it is appropriate for women to be just, it is necessary for both men and women to have learned these same most supreme and important things. When a man knows something about a craft that a woman doesn't know or if she knows something about a craft that a man doesn't, this does not demonstrate that the education of either one was different but that their training was. Rather than educating men and women differently concerning the most important things in life, we should teach them the same. If anyone asks me what knowledge guides this education, I will say to him that just as no man would be properly educated without philosophy, so no woman would be either. I am not advocating that women, if they study philosophy appropriately, should cultivate brilliance in arguments and an excessive cleverness: I don't approve this for men either. But women must develop good character and behave nobly, since indeed philosophy is nothing but the practice of noble behavior.

---

[35] There is a problem in the text here; I omit the problematic words.

5. From Lucius' notes on Musonius' lectures: Is practice or theory more important[36]

(1) On another occasion we asked him whether practice or theory is more effective for acquiring virtue, given that theory teaches what we ought to do and practice is demonstrated by those who have been trained to act in accordance with the theory. Musonius thought that practice was more effective, and in support of his own opinion he questioned one of the people present as follows: "Suppose there are two doctors. One of them can talk about medical matters as if he had the greatest possible acquaintance with them, but has never actually cared for sick people. The other is not able to talk about medical matters but is experienced in healing in accordance with medical theory. Which one would you choose as your doctor if you were ill?" His companion answered, "The one who is experienced in healing."

(2) Musonius then said: "Suppose there are two men, one of whom has sailed many times and has already piloted many boats, and the other of whom has sailed few times and has never been a pilot. Suppose the one who has never been a pilot can speak very fluently about the theory of navigation, and suppose the other speaks poorly and incoherently. Which would you hire as pilot if you were sailing?" And he said, "The one who has been a pilot many times."

(3) Again Musonius said: "Suppose there are two musicians. One understands musical theory and talks about it most fluently, but is not able to sing or to play the cithara or lyre. The other is ignorant of theory, but plays the cithara and lyre well and can sing. Which one would you want as a performer? Which one would you want as music teacher for a child ignorant of music?" He answered, "The one who is able to perform."

(4) "Given that this is so," said Musonius, "isn't being self-controlled and prudent about all one's actions much better than being able to say what is involved in prudence or self-mastery?" The young man agreed with this point—that speaking ably about self-control is less important and indeed is insignificant in comparison with actually being self-controlled. Then Musonius summarized his comments as follows: "How then would knowing the theory of a thing be better than practicing that theory and doing things in accordance with its

---

[36] Stobaeus 2.15.46. Chapter 15: about seeming and being and that one must judge a person not by word but by character, for without action all words are useless.

guidelines? Although understanding the theory behind the action enables one to speak, it is practice that enables one to act. Theory which teaches how one must act assists action and logically precedes practice, for it is not possible for something good to be accomplished unless it is accomplished in accordance with theory. But as a matter of fact, practice is more important than theory because it more effectively leads humans to actions than theory does."

6. By Musonius from the lecture on practicing philosophy[37]

(1) He gave lectures like this to his companions as he vigorously trained them in their practice of philosophy: virtue, he said, is not just theoretical knowledge, it is also practical, like both medical and musical knowledge. The doctor and the musician must each not only learn the principles of his own skill but be trained to act according to those principles. Likewise, the man who wants to be good must not only learn the lessons which pertain to virtue but train himself to follow them eagerly and rigorously.

(2) Could someone acquire instant self-control by merely knowing that he must not be conquered by pleasures but without training to resist them? Could someone become just by learning that he must love moderation but without practicing the avoidance of excess? Could we acquire courage by realizing that things which seem terrible to most people are not to be feared but without practicing being fearless towards them? Could we become wise by recognizing what things are truly good and what things are bad but without having been trained to look down on things which seem to be good?

(3) Therefore practicing each virtue always must follow learning the lessons appropriate to it, or it is pointless for us to learn about it. The person who claims to be studying philosophy must practice it even more diligently than the person who aspires to the art of medicine or some similar skill, inasmuch as philosophy is more important and harder to grasp than any other pursuit. People who study skills other than philosophy[38] have not been previously corrupted in their souls by learning things contrary to what they are about to learn, but people who attempt to study philosophy, since they have been already in the midst of much corruption and are filled with evil, pursue virtue in such a condition that they need even more practice in it.

(4) How, then, and in what way must they be trained? Since a human being happens to be neither soul alone nor body alone, but a composite of these two things, someone in training must pay attention to both. He should, rightly, pay more attention to the better part, namely the soul, but he should also take care of the other part, or part of him will become defective. The philosopher's body also must be well prepared for work because often virtues use it as a necessary tool

---

[37] Stobaeus 3.29.78. Chapter 29: about love of hard work.

[38] There is a textual problem here, and I omit the troublesome word.

for the activities of life. One type of training would be appropriate only for the soul, and another would be appropriate for both soul and body. We will train both soul and body when we accustom ourselves to cold, heat, thirst, hunger, scarcity of food, hardness of bed, abstaining from pleasures, and enduring pains.

(5) Through these methods and others like them, the body is strengthened, becomes inured to suffering, and strong and fit for every task; the soul is strengthened as it is trained for courage by enduring hardships and trained for self-control by abstaining from pleasures. The first step in the proper training of the soul is to keep handy the proofs showing that things which seem to be good are not good and that things which seem to be bad are not bad, and to become accustomed to recognizing things that are truly good and distinguishing them from things that are not. The next step is to be careful neither to flee from things that only seem to be bad nor to pursue things that only seem to be good, and then to avoid by all means things that are truly evil and in every way to strive to attain things that are truly good.

(6) To sum up, I have said enough about the character of each type of training. I will not attempt to explain in detail how each type should be done, and I will not distinguish or lay out which exercises are shared between soul and body and which apply to the soul alone. I will instead go through the exercises for each part in an unsystematic fashion. Indeed, those of us who have taken part in philosophical discussion obviously have heard and been exposed to the ideas that pain, death, poverty, and other things which are free of wickedness are in no way evil and, in turn, that wealth, life, pleasure or other things that have no share in virtue are not good. Nevertheless, even though we have heard these ideas, because of the corruption which has been ingrained in us all the way from childhood and because of the wicked behavior caused by this corruption, we think it a bad thing when pain comes on us, and we think it a good thing when pleasure comes.

(7) Likewise, we shudder at death as extreme misfortune, and we welcome life as the greatest good. When we give money away, we are distressed as if we are injured, and when we receive money, we rejoice as if we are helped. And in too many circumstances, we do not deal with our affairs in accordance with correct assumptions, but rather we follow thoughtless habit. Since I say that this is the case, the person who is practicing to become a philosopher must seek to overcome himself so that he won't welcome pleasure and avoid pain, so that he won't love living and fear death, and so that, in the case of money, he won't honor receiving over giving.

7. By Musonius, from the lecture on the subject that pain must be regarded as having little importance[39]

(1) In order for us to withstand more easily and eagerly the pains we would be suffering on account of virtue and noble character, it is useful to consider how much trouble those who pursue illicit love-affairs undergo because of their wicked passions, how much others put up with for the sake of gain, and again how many ills some suffer in pursuit of fame. And yet, all these people undergo all this hardship of their own accord. Is it not amazing that *they* would put up with all this on account of dishonorable things, but that *we*—to gain a noble character, to escape the wickedness that ruins our lives, and to acquire virtue which provides for all good things—would not readily withstand every pain?

(2) And yet, wouldn't everyone agree that it is much better to work to gain control over one's own desires than it is to work to gain possession of someone else's wife—and for a person to train himself to want little instead of struggling to become wealthy? And instead of exerting effort to gain fame, shouldn't a person strive to overcome his thirst for it? Instead of searching for a way to damage a person whom he envies, shouldn't he contemplate how not to bear envy against anyone? Instead of being slavish to some so-called friends, who are actually insincere, shouldn't he make sacrifices to win true friends?

(3) On the whole, since all people must endure pain, both those who seek better things and those who seek worse ones, it is quite strange that people who aim at the better things are not much more willing to endure pain than those who hope for little as a result of their efforts. Acrobats perform difficult feats, for example, and risk their own lives, some doing somersaults over knives, others walking high up on a tightrope, like birds flying through the air. A stumble is death for them, and yet they do all these things for little pay. Won't we, therefore, be willing to endure pain in order to gain complete happiness? For there is no other reason for becoming good than to be happy and live a blessed life thereafter.

(4) One might with reason consider some animals' ability to endure pain, and this ought to encourage us to do the same. Unlike humans, quails and cocks do not understand anything about virtue, do not know about beauty and justice, and do not seek these things; yet

---

[39] Stobaeus 3.29.75. Chapter 29: about love of hard work.

they fight against each other, keep on fighting even when injured, and fight to the death to avoid defeat.

(5) Isn't it more appropriate for us humans to endure and be strong? We understand, after all, that we suffer for the sake of something good, either to help our friends, to aid our city, to fight on behalf of women or children, or for the most important and weighty reason of all, to be good and just and self-controlled. No one achieves this without pain. And so I conclude that because we humans acquire all good things by pain, the person who is himself unwilling to endure pain all but condemns himself to being worthy of nothing good. He then continued in this vein, exhorting those present to regard pain as having little importance and spurring them on.

8. By Musonius, from the lecture showing that kings also should study philosophy[40]

(1) Once when one of the kings from Syria[41] came to him (for there were still kings in Syria then, subject to the Romans), he said to the man many things but especially the following: do not think, he said, that it is more appropriate for someone other than you to study philosophy, nor that it is more appropriate for you to study philosophy for any reason other than that you happen to be a king. Indeed a king must be able to keep his people safe and treat them well. The person who intends to protect and help people must know what is good for a human being and what is bad, what is helpful and what is harmful, what is useful and what is useless—since those who fall in with evil things are destroyed while those who get hold of good things are saved, and since those who are thought worthy of helpful and useful things do well while those who throw themselves among useless and harmful things do poorly.

(2) To diagnose good and evil, useful and useless, or helpful and harmful is the job of no one other than the philosopher. A philosopher has treated this very subject with the goal of not being ignorant of any one of these things and has made it his art to know what leads people to happiness or unhappiness. Therefore it seems to be necessary for a king to study philosophy. Indeed it is appropriate for a king—rather it is a necessity for him—to decide on just things for his subjects, so that no one has more or less than his due, but the ones who are deserving receive both honor and punishment.

(3) How would someone ever have this capability who was not just? How would anyone be just if he did not understand what sort of thing justice is? So again a king must study philosophy because

---

[40] Stobaeus 4.7.67. Chapter 7: advice about kingship.

[41] Rome controlled the Near East from the time of Pompey. Maurice Sartre in *The Middle East Under Rome* (Harvard 2005) uses "Middle East" to refer to "what is roughly the central part of the Near East, a region ancient authors would doubtless have designated by the umbrella term Syria" (p. 1). He means "the whole of the Semitic Near East between the Mediterranean and the Euphrates or the Syro-Arabian desert" (p. 2) and even Commagene. The province Syria was created by Pompey and kept being enlarged as the various client states in the region were taken over when their "kings" died. Client states which issued coins ("Herod and his successors, the Nabataeans, Commagene," p. 251) had rulers or kings. The last client king in this area was Rabbel II of the Nabataeans who died in AD 106 (p. 87). This lecture would have been written after that time, but we have no way of knowing what "Syrian" king Musonius talked to.

otherwise, it would not be clear that he knew about justice and what a just decision is. One must admit that someone who has studied just things will know them more thoroughly than someone who has not studied them—but also that people who have not studied philosophy are not entirely ignorant of such things. Indeed people argue and quarrel with each other about just things, some saying that these things are more just, others saying that those things are.

(4) And yet people do not disagree about things which they understand—about things that are white or black, hot or cold, soft or hard. All think and speak about these things with the same words. So they would think similarly also about just things if they knew what they were. Because they do not agree, they show that they are ignorant. And in my view, you are not free from this ignorance, and so you more than anyone else must pursue knowledge. Indeed, you must do this all the more because it is more shameful for a man who is a king to be ignorant of justice than it is for a private citizen.

(5) Furthermore, a king must himself be self-controlled and must control his subjects, so that he rules with self-control and they are ruled properly, in which case neither acts laxly. Laxness destroys everyone, both ruler and private citizen. How could someone be self-controlled himself if he does not practice mastering his desires? Or how could one who is self-indulgent make others exhibit self-control? What knowledge except philosophy draws one to self-control? One cannot name any. Philosophy teaches that we should be above pleasure and greed. It teaches that we should love frugality and avoid extravagance. It accustoms us to be modest and to control our tongue. It brings about discipline, order, decorum, and on the whole fitting behavior in action and in habit. If these things are present in a human being, they make him dignified and self-controlled. Any king who has these qualities would be most god-like and worthy of reverence.

(6) Being fearless, undaunted, and bold—these are the products of courage. And how else could these become someone's qualities more effectively than if he would become firmly convinced that death and pain are not evils? For death and pain are things which derange and frighten those who have been convinced that they are evils. Philosophy alone teaches that they are not evils. Consequently, if kings must possess courage—and they must possess it more than any other person—they must pursue the study of philosophy, since they could not become courageous in any other way.

(7) Also it is characteristic of kings, if nothing else, not to be bested in speech and to be able to prevail with words over those with

whom they speak just as they do with weapons over those with whom they fight. When kings are weak in this area, often they are of necessity perplexed and forced to accept false things as true; this is the result of a lack of sense and the result of extreme ignorance. Philosophy exists to provide those who study it with the ability to prevail in speech over those close by and to distinguish false things from true both by refuting the false and confirming the true. When orators enter into the same arena as philosophers and give and take in debate, it is possible to see them clashing with each other, and at a loss, being forced to say contradictory things. And yet when the orators, the people who have made it their business to study words, are exposed as being weaker in words than philosophers, how must other people fare? Therefore, if anyone who is a king wants power over speech, he must study philosophy so that he may not fear that anyone will be superior to him in this area. It is important for him not to fear this, since a king must be completely fearless and bold and unconquerable.

(8) On the whole, it is an absolute necessity that a good king be error-free and perfect in both word and deed, if indeed he must be the law that lives and breathes, as the men of old thought, bringing about good order and like-mindedness, preventing disorder and discord—and he must take Zeus as his role-model and like him be a father to those whom he rules. How could he be such a person if he is not supplied with an outstanding nature, having been given the best education and having all the virtues which are appropriate for a human being? If there is any knowledge other than philosophy which guides a person's nature towards virtue and teaches him to practice and associate with good things, it must be brought alongside and compared to see whether it or philosophy is better and more efficient at making a king good. A king who really wants to be good would with reason choose the better one.

(9) No other art promises the transmission and teaching of virtue. But there are arts which concern themselves with the human body and things useful for it. And other arts, though they deal with the soul, examine all things about it rather than how it will be self-controlled. Philosophy alone has the transmission and teaching of virtue as its goal and devises ways to help people escape wickedness and acquire virtue. If these things are so, what would be more important for a king who wants to be good than studying philosophy? How and in what way could one be a better king or live well without studying philosophy? I myself think that a good king is from the start a philosopher out of necessity, and that a philosopher is from the start also a kingly person.

(10) Let us start by considering the first of these claims. Is it possible that anyone could be a good king if he is not a good person? Clearly not. If someone is a good man, would he not be a philosopher too? Yes, by Zeus, if philosophy is the pursuit of nobility of character. And so a good king by necessity is found from the start to be a philosopher also. You could then learn that a philosopher is entirely kinglike from the following. It is surely characteristic of a kingly person to be able to govern peoples and cities well and to be worthy to rule over people. Who would be a more suitable leader of a city or more worthy to rule over people than a philosopher? It is appropriate for him (if he really is a philosopher) to be wise, self-controlled, magnanimous, a judge of just and proper things, able to accomplish what he sets out to do, and able to endure pain. In addition to these things, he should be bold, fearless, able to face things that seem terrible, and also a benefactor, honest, and humane. Who could be found more suitable to rule than such a man—or more capable? No one. Even though he lacks subjects who obey him, the philosopher is still kingly: for it is enough that he rules his friends, his wife and children, or even, by Zeus, just himself.

(11) A physician who heals a few people is a doctor no less than one who heals many, so long as he has medical skill. Likewise, a musician who teaches a few people is no less a musician than one who teaches many, so long as he has musical training. Similarly, a horse-trainer who trains one or two horses is just like one who trains many, so long as he is knowledgeable about training horses. And the person who has one or two people who obey him is kingly in the same way as one who possesses many subjects. Just give him the ability to rule, and as a result he would indeed be kingly. In my opinion this is why Socrates goes so far as to call philosophy the knowledge appropriate for a citizen and a king, because the person who takes it up is thereupon a proper citizen.

(12) When Musonius said things like these, the king was pleased by his words, confessed that he was grateful for what had been said to him, and said: "In return for these things, demand whatever you want from me, for I would not refuse you anything." Musonius replied: "I ask that you adhere to these principles and that you follow the words which you praise. In this way alone will you please me most and be most helped yourself."

9. By Musonius, from the lecture on why exile is not an evil thing[42]

(1) When an exiled person was complaining about his exile, Musonius gave him words of advice along the following lines. How, he asked, could any sensible person be upset by being in exile? Exile certainly does not deprive us of water, earth, air, or the sun and the other stars. Nor indeed does it deprive us of human companionship, for everywhere and in every way we have fellowship with other human beings. If we are removed from a certain part of the earth and from association with certain people, why is this terrible? Before our exile, we did not use all the earth, nor did we associate with all men. Even now in exile, we could associate with our friends—at least with those who are true and worthwhile. Such friends would never betray or abandon us. If some are insincere and false friends, we are better off being removed from them than associating with them.

(2) Well, isn't the world the common fatherland of all human beings, as Socrates thought? Consequently, you must not consider yourself to be exiled from your fatherland if you go away from where you were born and raised. Indeed, if you take yourself to be a reasonable person, you will instead conclude that you have been deprived only of a certain city. A reasonable person neither applauds a place nor rejects it because he holds it responsible for his happiness or unhappiness. He relies on himself for his whole well-being, and he considers himself to be a citizen of the city of Zeus which is populated by human beings and gods. Euripides also says similar things:

> The eagle can fly through all the air,
> and a noble man has all the earth as his fatherland.[43]

(3) A person who lives in his own country but in a different house from the one in which he was born, would be silly and ridiculous to

---

[42] Stobaeus 3.40.9. Chapter 40: about a foreign country.

[43] This is Euripides Fragment 1047 in the second edition of the fragments of writers of Greek tragedy (*Tragicorum Graecorum Fragmenta*, abbreviated *TGF*) collected by August Nauck (Leipzig: Teubner, 1889). We do not know what play the fragment comes from. Nauck's one book has now been replaced by six books with the same title, abbreviated *TrGF* (Göttingen: Vandenhoeck & Ruprecht, 1971–2004). Volume 5, published in 2004, is devoted to Euripides and had to be published in two parts. Its editor, R. Kannicht, maintained Nauck's numbering when he could; this fragment and the one in n. 45, below, have the same numbers as in Nauck.

complain and moan about this. Likewise, someone who thinks it a misfortune to be living in a different city from the one in which he happens to have been born could reasonably be considered to be witless and mindless. Indeed, how could exile preclude someone from caring for his real needs and from acquiring virtue? Exile, after all, never deprived anyone from learning what one needs to do and from acting accordingly. How could exile not help people work towards such a goal, since it provides them leisure and more opportunity to learn and do good things than they had before? In exile, after all, they are not dragged into political service by a country which only seems to be theirs. Nor are they bothered by people who only seem to be friends or by relatives who are good at keeping them preoccupied and distracting them from their search for better things.

(4) In fact, for some people exile has even been advantageous, all things considered. Exile transformed Diogenes from an ordinary person into a philosopher: instead of sitting around in Sinope, he spent his time in Greece, and in his practice of virtue he surpassed the other philosophers. Exile strengthened others who were unhealthy because of soft living and luxury: it forced them to follow a more manly lifestyle. We know that some were cured of chronic illnesses in exile. For example, Spartiatikos,[44] the Lacedaemonian, for a long time had a weak chest and because of this was often made sick by luxurious living. But when he stopped living like that, he regained his health. They say that others who indulged in soft living were cured of gout, even though they previously had been laid low by it. Exile, by accustoming them to live more austerely, restored their health. Thus, by improving people, exile helps them more than it hurts them with respect to both body and soul.

---

[44] Sparta was on Octavian's side during the war with Antony and Cleopatra. Antony had executed the Spartan Lachares (a pirate based on Cythera) who had sheltered Livia and her son Tiberius; the Claudii were patrons of Sparta (Livia and her husband were both Claudians). Lachares' son Eurycles contributed ships at Actium, became Spartan "ruler," and got Roman citizenship. He was exiled by Augustus (Octavian) probably as a result of his support of Tiberius in Tiberius' awkward sojourn at Rhodes. Tiberius installed Eurycles' son Laco as Spartan "ruler," but Laco was disgraced in the aftermath of Sejanus' fall; he was then reinstated at Sparta by either Gaius (Caligula) or Claudius. "The family's increased romanization . . . is shown by Claudius' grant of equestrian rank to Laco's son and heir, C. Iulius Spartiaticus," who himself was exiled (the evidence is this passage). The family continued but no longer as "rulers," and is last heard of under Hadrian. Paul Cartledge and Antony Spawforth, *Hellenistic and Roman Sparta: A Tale of Two Cities*, 2d ed. (Routledge 2002), pp. 97-112 (quoted material from p. 103; Spawforth is the author of this section); Nigel Kennell, *Spartans: A New History* (Wiley-Blackwell 2010), pp. 183-190.

(5) Exiles lack nothing essential. Those exiles who are lazy and shiftless—and who are unable to act like men even when they are not in exile—are generally at a loss and are without resources. But wherever noble, industrious, and intelligent men go, they flourish and do not feel deprived. Indeed we do not need many things unless we want to have a soft life—

> since what do mortals need except two things only,
> Demeter's grain and Aquarius' drink,
> things which are at hand and which exist to nourish us?[45]

(6) I say that men who are worthwhile not only would easily acquire the things most necessary for life when they are away from their home, but often would acquire many possessions as well. You must admit that Odysseus—alone, naked, and shipwrecked—was worse off than any exile. Nevertheless, when he arrived among the Phaeacians, who were unknown to him, he was able to acquire many possessions. When Themistocles was exiled from his home, he did not go to people who were friends; indeed, he went to the Persians, who were enemies and barbarians. They presented him with three cities—Myus, Magnesia, and Lampsacus—from which he derived his living expenses. When Dion the Syracusan was robbed of all his property by Dionysius the tyrant and was thrown out of his fatherland, he got hold of so much money in his exile that he formed a mercenary army with which he invaded Sicily and freed it from the tyrant. What sensible person who considers these examples would still suppose that exile itself is what creates difficulties for those who are exiled?

---

[45] Euripides Fragment 892 in Nauck's second edition. (See n. 43, above.) This is quoted by several other writers, and they vouch for its attribution to Euripides. There are two more lines:

> Abundance of these things does not satisfy. Indeed in our luxurious living
> we track down ways to get other things to consume.

Athenaeus, *Learned Banqueters* 4.158e (Loeb Classical Library, 2006), edited and translated by S. Douglas Olson, and Aulus Gellius, *Attic Nights* 6.16.7 (n. 10, above), quote all five lines and attribute them to Euripides. The Stoic Chrysippus liked to cite them. Plutarch criticizes him for this in "Stoic Self-Contradictions," *Moralia* 1043 E, 1044 B and F; he uses only the first three lines: Loeb, vol XIII, Part II, edited and translated by Harold Cherniss, 1976. Again we do not know what play this fragment comes from. Athenaeus was active about AD 200; his work is set at a banquet, and the learned guests banter quotations from "great" authors back and forth. Like Stobaeus, Athenaeus is a major source for material from lost works.

(7) Exiles need not get a bad reputation because of being exiled. Everyone knows, after all, that many cases are judged wrongly, that many people are thrown out of their fatherland unjustly, and that some men who were good have been driven out by their fellow citizens. Aristides the Just, for example, was exiled from Athens, and Hermodorus was exiled from Ephesus.[46] (And when Hermodorus was exiled, Heraclitus even ordered Ephesian adults to hang themselves.) Indeed some exiles became very famous: for example, Diogenes of Sinope, Clearchus the Lacedaemonian—the one who marched with Cyrus against Artaxerxes—and one could mention many others if one wished. How indeed could exile itself impair one's reputation? During their exile, some people have become more famous than they were before.

(8) But, by Zeus, Euripides says that exiles have been deprived of liberty inasmuch as they have lost their freedom of speech: in the *Phoenician Women*, he has Jocasta ask her son Polynices what things are hard to bear for an exile, and he answers that:

> one thing is very great, that he does not have freedom of speech.[47]

She in turn says to him:

> not saying what one thinks—this is the condition of a slave which you describe.[48]

I would say to Euripides: "O Euripides, you describe a slave's situation correctly—not saying what he thinks when he should speak. Indeed, we should not say what we think always, everywhere, and to anyone at all. But I think you are mistaken about the point that exiles lack freedom of speech, if by freedom of speech you mean not keeping quiet about what one happens to think. People do not refrain from saying what they think because they are exiles; they refrain because they fear that they will suffer pain, death, penalty, or some other such thing for speaking. By Zeus, it is not exile but fear that silences people. Those who still live in their own country—most people, that is—fear things

---

[46] Cicero discusses the exile of Hermodorus in *Tusculan Disputations* 5.36.105: Heraclitus said that all the Ephesians should be put to death for their rationale for having exiled Hermodorus: they wanted no one person to be superior to the rest, and Hermodorus was simply too outstanding.

[47] Euripides, *Phoenician Women*, 391.

[48] Euripides, *Phoenician Women*, 392.

that seem dangerous. The courageous man is as courageous in exile as he was at home; therefore he also says as boldly what he thinks when exiled as when he was not an exile." One could say these things to Euripides.

(9) But, my friend, tell me, when Diogenes was in exile at Athens or when he was grabbed by bandits and went to Corinth, did anyone else, whether Athenian or Corinthian, then display more freedom of speech than Diogenes? Absolutely not. Who at that time was freer than Diogenes? He ruled even Xeniades, who bought him, as a master rules a slave. But why must I resort to historical examples? Don't you know that I myself am an exile? Have I been robbed of free speech? Have I had the power of saying what I think taken from me? Have you or anyone else seen me crouching before anyone because I am an exile, or have you seen me thinking that my condition is worse than before? By Zeus, you must admit that you have never seen me groaning or moaning because of my exile. Even if someone has deprived us of our country, he has not taken away our ability to endure exile.

(10) Let me tell you how I convince myself not to be bothered by exile. As I showed you above, I do not think that exile completely deprives a person of the things which many people consider good. And even if it would deprive a person of some or all of these things, it does not deprive him of things that are truly good. The person in exile is not prevented from having courage, justice, self-control, wisdom, or any other virtue, just because he is in exile. When these qualities are present, they tend to honor and benefit a person and show him to be deserving of praise and fame. The absence of these qualities works to harm and shame him by showing him to be bad and without fame. Consequently, if you are a good and virtuous person, exile would not harm or diminish you, because you still have the things that can best assist and elevate you. And if you happen to be a bad person, it is vice, not exile, that harms you—vice, not exile, that brings you grief. You must work on freeing yourself from vice rather than from exile.

(11) These things I used to say to myself repeatedly, and I now say them to you as well. If you are wise, you will not consider exile to be a terrible thing (since others bear it easily), but you will consider evil to be a terrible thing: when evil is present, everyone afflicted by it is miserable. Indeed, one of two things must be the case: you are in exile either unjustly or justly. If justly, how is it correct or proper to be upset over just things? If unjustly, our exile is caused not by our wickedness but by the wickedness of the people who sent us into exile. (And in this case *they* are wicked, since, by Zeus, acting unjustly—the thing

which has befallen them—is the thing most hated by the gods.) Both the gods and fair-minded men will agree that those who have been wronged—those like ourselves—deserve help, not hatred.

10. By Musonius, from the lecture on whether a philosopher will file a suit against someone for assault[49]

(1) He said that he would never file a lawsuit against anyone for assault; nor would he advise anyone who thinks that the study of philosophy is worthwhile to file one. Consider the things people think they are injured by when they experience them; none of these things will in fact injure them or cause them shame. These things include being jeered at, beaten, or spat upon, with assaults being the worst of these outrages. When they are whipped in public and revel in being whipped, Spartan boys make it clear that such things are neither shameful nor injurious. If a philosopher cannot scorn blows or jeering, he is useless, inasmuch as a philosopher must make it clear that he scorns even death.

(2) "But, by Zeus, the person who does these things—who mocks and thinks that he is committing outrage by slapping, jeering, or doing some such thing—has hostile intent! Indeed, Demosthenes believes that people can insult with a mere glance, that such glances are unbearable, and that, somehow or other, people lose control because of them."

(3) Those who do not know what is really good and what is really shameful, and who are overly concerned with their own fame—these people think that they are being injured if someone glares at them, laughs at them, hits them, or mocks them. But a man who is thoughtful and sensible—as a philosopher should be—is disturbed by none of these things. He believes that the shame comes not in being insulted but in behaving in an insulting manner. What wrong does the person who experiences wrong do? The person who does wrong, however, is thereby shamed. But since the person who is wronged does not thereby do wrong, he is not thereby shamed. Consequently, a sensible person would not resort to lawsuits or indictments since he would not think that he had been insulted. Indeed, it is petty to be vexed or put out about such things. He will calmly and quietly bear what has happened, since this is appropriate behavior for a person who wants to be magnanimous.

(4) Socrates obviously refused to be upset when he was publicly ridiculed by Aristophanes; indeed, when Socrates met Aristophanes, he asked if Aristophanes would like to make other such use of him. It is

---

[49] Stobaeus 3.19.16. Chapter 19: about putting up with evil.

unlikely that this man would have become angry if he had been the target of some minor slight, since he was not upset when he was ridiculed in the theater! Phocion the Good,[50] when his wife was insulted by someone, didn't even consider bringing charges against the insulter. In fact, when that person came to him in fear and asked Phocion to forgive him, saying that he did not know that it was his wife whom he offended, Phocion replied: "My wife has suffered nothing because of you, but perhaps some other woman has. So you don't need to apologize to me."

(5) And I could name many other men who were targets of abuse, some verbally attacked and others injured by physical attacks. They appear neither to have defended themselves against their attackers nor to have sought revenge. Instead, they very calmly bore the wrong committed by their attackers. Indeed, plotting how to bite back someone who bites and to return evil against the one who first did evil is characteristic of a beast, not a man. A beast is not able to comprehend that many of the wrongs done to people are done out of ignorance and a lack of understanding. A person who gains this comprehension immediately stops doing wrong.

(6) It is characteristic of a civilized and humane temperament not to respond to wrongs as a beast would and not to be implacable towards those who offend, but to provide them with a model of decent behavior. A philosopher who thinks it right to forgive someone who offends him and acts accordingly is obviously better than one who thinks that he must defend himself by filing lawsuits and indictments, but who in fact is disgracing himself by doing things inconsistent with his own teachings. A philosopher is, after all, inconsistent if he says that a good man could never be wronged by a bad man, but then, while claiming to be a good man, charges that he is wronged by bad men.

---

[50] Phocion was an Athenian politician of the fourth century BC. He was elected *stratēgos* ("general") forty-five times.

11. By Musonius, from the lecture, "What is the suitable occupation for a philosopher?"[51]

(1) There is another occupation no worse than this, and perhaps one might reasonably consider that it is even better for a man strong in body—namely, earning one's living from the land, if one owns some, and, indeed, even if one doesn't. Many of those who farm someone else's land, whether publicly or privately owned, are able to support not only themselves but also their children and wives. Because they work with their own hands and are industrious, some earn a very good living this way. The earth repays most beautifully and justly those who care for her, giving back many times what she receives. For someone willing to work, she supplies an abundance of all the things necessary for life and does so in a seemly and shame-free manner.

(2) Only someone decadent or soft would say that agricultural tasks are shameful or unsuitable for a good man. How could planting trees, plowing, and working with vines not be a good thing? Aren't sowing, harvesting, and threshing all compatible with freedom and suitable for good men? Just as being a shepherd did not shame Hesiod or keep him from being loved by both the gods and muses, so it would hinder no one else.

(3) To me, this is the main benefit of all agricultural tasks: they provide abundant leisure for the soul to do some deep thinking and to reflect on the nature of education. Tasks that stretch and bend the whole body force the soul to be focused on them alone or on the body alone. Tasks that don't require excessive physical exertion don't prevent the soul from contemplating the better things and thus from becoming wiser than it was—which is the goal of every philosopher. Because of this, I very much approve of the shepherd's life. But if a person studies philosophy and farms at the same time, I would not offer any other way of life to him; nor would I advocate another occupation.

(4) Isn't it more in accordance with nature to be nourished from the earth, which is both our nurse and mother, than from some other source? Isn't living in the country more suitable for a man than sitting in the city like the sophists? Isn't living outside more healthy than being secluded in the shade? What is more characteristic of a free person than that he provide necessities for himself rather than receive them

---

[51] Stobaeus 4.15a.18. Chapter 15: about farming. Part A: about farming—that it is a good thing.

from others? Clearly, not having to ask someone else to provide for one's needs is much more seemly than having to ask. Consequently, earning one's living from farming is noble, blessed, and god-favored, as is paying attention to nobility of character. For this reason, the god declared that Myson of Chen[52] was wise and announced that Aglaos of Psophis[53] was blessed; they lived in the country, worked with their own hands, and avoided spending time in the city. Isn't it worthwhile both to praise and imitate them and to embrace farming with zeal?

(5) But someone might say: "Isn't it a terrible thing for an educated man—one who is able to introduce young people to philosophy—to work the land and engage in manual labor like country people?" Yes, this would really be terrible if working the land prevented him from doing philosophy or helping others to do philosophy. But I think that young people would benefit less by being with their teacher in the city or by listening to him speak in a formal presentation than they do by watching him work in the country and actually do what reason teaches us to do—namely, to work and endure pain ourselves rather than ask someone else to support us. What, after all, prevents the pupil who is working with his teacher from simultaneously listening to him speak about self-control, justice, or bravery? Those who want to do philosophy properly do not need many words. Nor do young people need to absorb the multitude of theories that we see sophists inflating themselves with—theories that truly are enough to consume a man's life. Those who do farm work can learn the most essential and useful things, especially if they will not be working all the time but can take some breaks. I fully realize that few people will want to learn in this way, but it is better for most of the young people who claim to be studying philosophy not to go near a philosopher—at least not those philosophers who are decadent and soft, and by whom, when they come near, philosophy is tainted.

(6) All true lovers of philosophy would be willing to spend time in the country with a good man, even if the place happened to be quite

---

[52] The obscure Myson of Chen was substituted for the tyrant Periander of Corinth in Plato's list of the traditional seven sages (*Protagoras* 343a). See David Berger, "Periander the Wise?" *New England Classical Journal* 34 (2007): 22–35, especially 24–25. The location of Chen has not been determined, so perhaps Plato is making a joke: *chēn* is the Greek word for "wild goose."

[53] The even more obscure Aglaos of Psophis is mentioned in Pliny the Elder's *Natural History* 7.46.151 and Valerius Maximus 7.2 as the oracle's response to Gyges of Lydia who asked about the happiest man. Psophis was in Arcadia; Aglaos was an old man who had never left his farm.

primitive. He would, after all, benefit greatly from the time he spends there by being with his teacher night and day and by being away from those urban evils that interfere with the study of philosophy. He would also be unable to conceal whether he is doing something well or badly, which is highly beneficial for those who are being educated. Likewise, to eat, drink, and sleep while being observed by a good man is very beneficial. These things, which would necessarily result from being together in the country, Theognis also praises:

> Drink and eat and sit with them
> whose power is great and please them too.[54]

Theognis also makes it clear that only good men can greatly benefit those who eat, drink, and sit with them:

> From good men you will learn good things. If you mix with bad men,
> you will destroy even your existing sense.[55]

Indeed, don't let anyone say that farming gets in the way of learning or teaching essential things. This is unlikely to happen as long as the student can be with the teacher and interact in the manner described above for as long as possible. Under these circumstances, farming seems to be the ideal occupation for a philosopher.

---

[54] Theognis, lines 33–34, in *Greek Elegiac Poetry*, edited and translated by Douglas E. Gerber (Loeb Classical Library, 1999).

[55] Theognis, lines 35–36.

12. By Musonius, from the lecture about sexual matters[56]

(1) A significant part of luxurious living involves sexual behavior, because men who live luxuriously desire a variety of sexual experiences, both legitimate and illegitimate, and with both women and men. Sometimes, they pursue one male as their beloved, sometimes another. Sometimes they are not satisfied with those males who are available but go after the ones who are hard to get, and seek unseemly embraces. All of these actions are great reproaches against a human being. Men who are neither licentious nor wicked must consider only those sexual acts which occur in marriage and which are carried out for the creation of children to be right, since these acts are also lawful, but they must consider acts that chase after mere pleasure, even if they occur in marriage as wrong and unlawful.

(2) Among other sexual relationships, the most illegitimate involve adultery, and the relationships in which males relate to males are no more tolerable than adulterous ones because this outrage is contrary to nature. Unlawful relationships with women, even if they do not involve adultery, are all of them shameful since they are undertaken out of a lack of self-control. For example, no one with self-control would decide to associate with a mistress, with a free woman outside of marriage, or even, by Zeus, with his own female slave. The illegal and improper aspect of these relationships makes them a disgrace and a great reproach to men who pursue them. And so no one capable of blushing even a little dares to do any of these things openly. Unless they are completely dissolute, they cover up what they are doing and embark on these affairs only in secrecy. And yet, trying to hide what someone does is a sign that one knows that what one is doing is wrong.

(3) "By Zeus," says a listener, "even though the adulterer wrongs the husband of the seduced woman, the man who associates with a mistress or even, by Zeus, with an unmarried woman does not wrong anyone, for he does not ruin anyone's hope for legitimate heirs." I maintain, however, that everyone who acts wrongly and unjustly, even if he doesn't hurt those near to him, immediately shows himself to be entirely base and somewhat dishonorable. The person who does wrong, inasmuch as he does wrong, is base and dishonorable. Even if we ignore the unjust behavior, we must conclude that the man

---

[56] Stobaeus 3.6.23. Chapter 6: on self-indulgence.

overcome by shameful pleasure—the man who delights in getting himself dirty, as pigs do—is controlled by his lack of self-control.

(4) This includes the man who consorts with his own female slave, an act some people consider to be completely blameless, since every master is thought to have complete power to use his own slave however he wants. In response to this, my reasoning is simple: if someone thinks that it is neither shameful nor unnatural for a master to consort with his own female slave (and especially if she happens to be unmarried), what would he think if his wife would consort with a male slave? Would he not think that this was intolerable, not just if a woman who had a lawful husband would submit to a male slave, but even if an unmarried woman would do this? And yet, no one will suggest that men should have a lower standard of conduct than women or be less able to discipline their own desires—that those who are supposedly stronger in wisdom would be bested by those who are weaker, or that those who are rulers would be bested by those who are ruled! Men should have a much higher standard of behavior if they expect women to follow them. If they are more weak-willed than women, they appear inferior to them. Why do I even need to say that only a lack of self-control could cause a master to consort with a female slave? Everyone knows this.

13. By Musonius, from the lecture, "What is the chief end of marriage?"[57]

Part A[58]

(1) He said that the chief end of marriage is uniting to live together and have children. Husband and wife should come together for the following reasons: to live with each other, to have children, and to consider all things as common possessions and nothing as private—not even the body itself. The birth of the child which this union[59] will bring about is important. But this cannot be the only motive for marriage since procreation could result from sexual relations apart from marriage, just as when animals mate.

(2) In marriage there must be, above all, companionship and care of husband and wife for each other, both in sickness and in health and on every occasion. Each party entering into a marriage desires this, after all, just as they desire children. When this mutual care is complete and those who live together provide it to each other completely, each competes to surpass the other in giving such care. Such a marriage is admirable and deserves emulation; such a partnership is beautiful.

(3) Sometimes a spouse considers only his or her own interests and neglects the other's concerns. Sometimes, by Zeus, a husband who acts like this lives in the same house as his wife but concentrates on matters outside of it, and is unwilling to work with, let alone agree with her.[60] In cases like this, even though the couple lives together, their union is bound to be destroyed and their affairs cannot help but go poorly: they either break apart completely from each other, or they have a relationship that is worse than solitude.

---

[57] The excerpts in Stobaeus have the same title and come from the same lecture, but Stobaeus chose them to fit *his* categories. We have no way of knowing what he left out.

[58] Stobaeus 4.22c.90. Chapter 22: about marriage. Part c: that the character of those embarking on marriage makes it a benefit to some, but a misfortune to others.

[59] *zeugos*, meaning "yoke, yoking, pairing."

[60] to pull (the yoke) with and to breathe along with his yoke-mate.

Part B[61]

(1) Those who plan to marry must not concern themselves with finding partners who come from noble families or who have great wealth or beautiful bodies. Neither wealth nor beauty nor noble birth have been able to increase a sense of partnership, let alone increase harmony; nor do they aid the creation of children. Bodies best fitted for marriage are healthy, normal in form, and able to function on their own. Such bodies would be less likely to be ensnared by people who lack self-control and would be more able to carry out the body's functions and produce children without difficulty.

(2) Souls that are naturally disposed towards self-control and justice—in a word, towards virtue—are obviously most suitable for marriage. Could a marriage be good without harmony? Could such a union be noble? Could wicked people be in harmony with each other? Could a good person be in harmony with a bad one? This could not happen, any more than a crooked piece of wood could fit together with a similar crooked one or than two crooked pieces could fit together. (The crooked piece would not fit together with another similarly crooked piece and would fit even worse with its opposite, a straight piece.) A wicked man does not befriend a wicked man and does not get along with him. And a wicked man finds it even harder to get along with a good man.

---

[61] Stobaeus 4.22d.104. Part d: on courtship.

14. By Musonius, from the lecture about whether marriage gets in the way of studying philosophy[62]

(1) When someone said that marriage and life with a wife seemed to him to get in the way of studying philosophy, Musonius said that marriage did not hinder Pythagoras or Socrates or Crates, each of whom lived with a wife, and no one could name other philosophers who were better than these. Even though Crates had no home, property, or money, he nevertheless married, and since he did not have a place of his own, he passed his days and nights with his wife in the public stoas at Athens. Are we who have a house and maybe even servants who wait on us nevertheless so bold as to claim that marriage gets in the way of studying philosophy?

(2) Indeed, the philosopher is doubtless a teacher and guide regarding what human beings must do to be in accordance with nature. Marriage obviously is in accordance with nature, if anything is. Why else did the creator of humankind first cut our species into two and then make for it two sets of genitals, one female, one male? Why else did he then implant in each a strong desire for companionship and union with the other and mix into both a strong longing for the other, the male for the female and the female for the male? Is it not obvious that he wanted the two to be together, live together, and work together in daily life, and together provide for the birth of children and their upbringing, so that our species may be everlasting?

(3) Tell me, then, shouldn't everyone do things for his neighbor as well as for himself and thus make sure that his city has thriving families and that it is not a wasteland? Isn't this how commonwealths thrive? To say that each should look only to his own affairs is to admit that a human being is no different from a wolf or any of the other wildest beasts whose nature it is to live by force and greed. They spare nothing that they can devour, they have no share in companionship, they take no part in working with each other, and they have no share in anything just. But you will agree that human nature is very much like that of bees. A bee is not able to live alone: it perishes when isolated. Indeed, it is intent on performing the common task of members of its species—to work and act together with other bees. Given that this is so, and given, too, that a wicked person displays injustice and

---

[62] Stobaeus 4.22a.20. Chapter 22: about marriage. Part A: that marriage is a very good thing.

savageness, as well as a lack of concern for a neighbor in trouble, while a virtuous person displays love for his fellow human beings, as well as goodness, justice, kindness, and concern for his neighbor—given all this, shouldn't each person, out of concern for his city, create a family with the well-being of the city in mind? And marriage is the way for the family to provide this well-being.

(4) Anyone who deprives people of marriage destroys family, city, and indeed, the whole human race. Humans would cease to exist if there were no procreation, and there would not be procreation without marriage—just and lawful procreation, that is. Clearly, families and cities do not arise from women or from men alone, but from their union with each other. One could not find a union more necessary or agreeable than the union of men and women. What man feels so close to his male friend as a devoted wife feels to her husband? What brother feels so close to his brother? What son feels so close to his parents? Who is missed so much when absent as a husband is by his wife or a wife is by her husband? Whose presence could do more to lessen grief, increase joy, or alleviate misfortune?

(5) By whom, if not by husband and wife, is it right for all things—bodies, souls, and possessions—to be held in common? Surely it is for this reason that everyone considers the love of a husband and wife to be the most honorable of all loves, and no sensible mother or father would think it right to be dearer to his or her own children than to the one joined to him or her in marriage. The following story shows clearly how much the love of a wife for her husband exceeds that of parents for children. Admetus received as a gift from the gods that he would live for double the time allotted to him if he could provide a person who would die in his place. He found that his parents were not willing to die in his place, even though they were aged. But his wife, although quite young, readily accepted death in place of her husband.

(6) Another reason marriage is important and should be taken seriously is that gods govern it—great gods who are worshiped by human beings. First there is Hera, who we say joins the pair together. Then comes Eros, then Aphrodite. We believe that these gods are in charge of bringing a man and woman together for procreation. And where would the presence of Eros, Hera, and Aphrodite be more appropriate than at the lawful union of man and woman? What more auspicious time would there be to pray to these gods than when getting married? What more appropriate function would Aphrodite have than to join wife with husband? Why would anyone say that such great gods guard and govern marriage and procreation, but that human

beings don't care about these activities? And if any human cares about them, won't philosophers? After all, can a philosopher be worse than other people? Certainly not! He must be better, more just, and more noble in character than they are.

(7) Isn't a person who does not concern himself with his own city worse and less just than someone who does? Isn't the person who looks only after his own interest worse than the one who takes the common good into consideration? Does the person who chooses a solitary life love his city, his fellow man, and the common good more than the man who sets up a household, has children, and helps his own city grow—all activities which characterize a married man? It is clear that the proper concern of the philosopher is marriage and procreation. If these are proper concerns, my young friend, how could the claim that you just made—that marriage gets in the way of a philosopher—be correct? After all, to practice philosophy is obviously to use reason to determine what actions are seemly and appropriate, and then to do them. This is how he spoke then.

15. By Musonius, from the lecture on whether all children who are born must be raised

Part A[63]

(1) The lawgivers—whose job it was to research and consider what is good for a city and what is bad, what benefits the common good and what harms it—didn't they all consider it most beneficial for cities that citizens' households be increased and most harmful for cities that these households be diminished? Didn't they think it unprofitable for citizens to have few or no children, and didn't they think it profitable for them to have children and even, by Zeus, to have a lot of them? Because they thought this, they forbade women from inducing miscarriages and established punishment for those who disobeyed, they forbade women from agreeing to be childless and from preventing conception, they honored married couples who had a lot of children, and they punished those who were childless.

(2) Wouldn't we therefore be doing unjust and unlawful things if we acted contrary to the intention of the lawgivers—men who were godlike and beloved by the gods, and whom we must consider it right and advantageous to follow? We would be acting contrary to their intention if we prevented ourselves from having a lot of children. By doing this, wouldn't we be wronging both our ancestral gods and Zeus, who guards the family? The person who is unjust towards strangers wrongs Zeus, the guardian of strangers, and the person who is unjust towards his friends wrongs Zeus, the god of friendship. Likewise, the person who is unjust towards his own family wrongs his ancestral gods and Zeus, the protector of families who takes note of crimes connected with families. Anyone who wrongs the gods is impious.

(3) Indeed, to see that raising many children is a right and profitable thing to do, one need only take note of how honored in his city is the man with many children, how he earns respect from his neighbors, and how much more power he has than his less-prolific peers. Just as, I think, the man who has a lot of friends is more powerful than the man who has none, the man who has a lot of children is much more

---

[63] Stobaeus 4.24a.15. Chapter 24: about children. Part A: that having children is a good thing. (P.Harris 1 covered all of this excerpt and continued beyond for several lines.)

powerful still than the man who has few or none. This power is a consequence of a son's being closer to a man than a friend is.

(4) Here is another noteworthy point: what a great spectacle it is when a husband or wife with many children are seen with these children crowded around them! No procession conducted for the gods is as beautiful to look at, and no ritual performed solemnly for a sacred occasion is as worthy of being watched, as is a chorus of many children guiding their parents through the city, leading them by the hand or otherwise caring for them. What is more lovely than this spectacle? What is more worthy of emulation than these parents, especially if they are decent people? What other people would we join with so eagerly in praying for good things from the gods? What other people, indeed, would we help obtain whatever they might need?

(5) "By Zeus," asks a listener, "but[64] if I am poor and lack money and I possess many children, how could I raise all of them?" Musonius replies: "How do these little birds—the swallows and nightingales and larks and blackbirds—which have far fewer resources than you raise their own nestlings? In the *Iliad* Homer speaks of them thus:

> As a bird carries to her nestlings which cannot fly
> a morsel whenever she gets it, and she gets very little[65]

Do these creatures outdo a human being in wit? This is unlikely. What then? In strength and force? This is even less likely. What then? Do they store away food and guard it?"

Part B[66]

(1) I think it completely outrageous that some who are not even able to use poverty as an excuse, but who are well-off or even rich, refuse to raise children who are born later so that the earlier-born ones may be better off; they ensure the prosperity of these first-born children by means of an unholy act. They deprive them of brothers so that they might have a greater share of their father's possessions. They

---

[64] The rest of this paragraph comes from P.Harris 1. I follow Lutz's text which incorporates emendations made by others to Powell's original publications.

[65] Homer, *Iliad*, 9.323–4.

[66] Stobaeus 4.27.21. Chapter 27: that a very good thing is brotherly love as well as regard for blood-relatives and that they are necessary.

fail to appreciate how much better it is to have many brothers than to have many possessions.

(2) This is because possessions invite plots from neighbors, and brothers forestall these plotters. Furthermore, these possessions need protection, and your brothers are your greatest protectors. You could not compare a good friend to a brother nor could you compare the protection provided by other people, even those like themselves, to the protection provided by brothers.[67] What good thing could you compare to the good will of a brother for guaranteeing your security? Who could more graciously share life's blessings with you than a kind brother? Whose presence could you want more in troubled times than such a brother's?

(3) I myself think that the man who lives with many loyal brothers is most worthy of emulation, and I think that the man who enjoys these blessings is most beloved by the gods. Therefore I think that we should try to leave our children brothers rather than possessions, in order to give them greater chances for blessings.

---

[67] There is a problem and gap in the text. I am translating *parabaloi an tis oute boethian* and deleting *ton*; *para* is in the text.

16. By Musonius, from the lecture on whether parents must be obeyed in all things[68]

(1) A young man who wanted to study philosophy but whose father was keeping him from doing so questioned Musonius like this: "Musonius, is it always necessary to obey parents, or are there some situations in which one should disobey?" Musonius replied: "It is obviously a good thing for children to obey their mother or father, and I myself approve of this. Yet let us see what it means to obey. Rather let us first examine what disobedience is and who is in fact disobedient; then we will better understand the nature of disobedience."

(2) Consider, then, a father who is neither a doctor nor acquainted with matters pertaining to health and sickness. Suppose he ordered something for his sick son that he thought would help but which was useless, if not harmful. Suppose, too, that the sick son knew this. If the son did not do what was ordered, is he disobeying his father and is he disobedient? This is unlikely.

(3) Or, suppose that the father himself was the sick one and would ask for wine or food he wasn't supposed to have—things which, if he consumed them, would make his sickness worse. If the son knew this and refused to give them to him, is he disobeying his father? Of course not.

(4) And even less disobedient than this son is a son who, when his greedy father orders him to steal or to embezzle money entrusted to him, refuses to do so. Don't you think there are fathers who give their children such orders? I myself know a man who had a remarkably beautiful son and who was so wicked that he put his son's beauty up for sale. If that youth who was sold and sent by his father into shame had refused and had not gone, would we say that the youth was disobedient—or would we say that he was being modest? It is not decent even to ask this, is it?

(5) It is true that the act of disobeying and the person who disobeys are shameful and blameworthy. But refusing to do what one should not do brings praise, not shame. And so, if someone refuses to obey a person who is doing something wicked, unjust, or shameful—whether that person is his father, a ruler, or even, by Zeus, a despot—

---

[68] Stobaeus 4.25.51. Chapter 25: that parents must be considered worthy of appropriate respect from their children and whether they must be obeyed in all things.

he is not disobeying, and he certainly isn't being unjust or doing something wrong. A disobedient person is one who ignores or disobeys orders that are right, honorable, and beneficial. *That* is what a disobedient person is.

(6) The obedient person behaves in the opposite way and is different from the disobedient one. He would listen to someone who gives appropriate advice and follow it willingly. He obeys his parents when he willingly follows the good advice they give; and when they don't give good advice, I say that he is nevertheless obeying his parents when he does what he should and what benefits himself. In support of this claim, consider the following. The person who does what his father wants and follows his father's wish is obeying his father, of course. But the person who does what he should and what it is better for him to do also follows his father's wish. How can this be? Because all parents want the best for their children, and since they do, they want them to do what they should do and what benefits them. Consequently, anyone who does what is appropriate and beneficial is doing what his parents want—he is obeying his parents, even if his parents do not explicitly tell him what to do. Anyone who wants to obey his parents in all of his actions need only consider whether what he intends to do is good and useful, and nothing else. If one follows this principle, he is obeying his parents.

(7) So, young man, don't worry that you will be disobeying your father, if you refuse to do the inappropriate things he orders you to do or if you do appropriate things he forbids you to do. Don't use your father as an excuse for doing wrong, when he either orders you to do something that is wrong or forbids you to do something that is right. You needn't follow orders that are not right. I think you realize this. If your father does not understand music and he tells you to pluck the lyre in a discordant manner, you won't obey. If you are literate and he is not, and he orders you to write and read in a manner you know to be incorrect, you won't obey. Likewise, if you know how to steer, you won't listen when someone who isn't a steersman gives you incorrect orders. This much is clear.

(8) If your father, who knows nothing about philosophy, prevents you from studying it, but you know and understand what it is, should you listen to him? Or should you instead explain to him that he is not giving you good advice? You should do the latter, I think. If one's father is not completely hard-headed, a son might even use reason to persuade him of the value of studying philosophy. If the father is

impervious to reason and unmoved by it, the actions of a son who is truly pursuing philosophy will convince him of its value. As a student of philosophy, he will be most eager to help his father in every way, and he will be conspicuously self-disciplined and courteous. In his dealings with his father, he will never be quarrelsome or self-regarding, and never rash, rebellious, or angry. Furthermore, he would be in control of his tongue, stomach, and sexual appetites, and would be brave enough to face calamities and pain. Likewise, he will be well-equipped to recognize what is right and won't be deceived by what only seems right. He will gladly forsake all pleasures for his father and for him will shoulder hardships. Who would not pray to the gods to have such a son? And who, if he had such a son, would not love him? All sensible people would envy a father with such a son and call that father blessed.

(9) But suppose, young man, that even the prospect of your becoming such a son if you truly pursue philosophy will not win your father over or persuade him to give in and let you study it. In that case, consider that, although your father forbids you to study philosophy, Zeus, the common father of all, both humans and gods, orders and encourages you to do it. His commandment and law is that a human being be just, righteous, kind, self-controlled, magnanimous, above pain and pleasure, and devoid of all envy and treachery. Stated briefly, the law of Zeus orders the human being to be good, and being good is the same thing as being a philosopher. If you obey your father, you will be following a human being, but if you pursue philosophy, you will be following Zeus. It is therefore clear that you should choose to study philosophy.

(10) But, by Zeus, you say that your father will restrain you and keep you shut up to prevent you from studying philosophy. Even if he does this, he will not prevent you from studying it unless you let him. We do not seek philosophy with hand, foot, or any other body part, but with our soul and that little part of it we call our intellect. Zeus planted this securely within us, in a place where it cannot be seen and touched, and where it is autonomous and unconstrained. Besides, if your intellect is keen, your father will not be able to prevent you from using it or from drawing proper conclusions. Nor will he be able to prevent you from using it to be pleased by the good rather than by the shameful, or from choosing the good and refusing the shameful. If you do these things, you would be studying philosophy anyway. You won't

need to don an old cloak, go around without a *chiton*,[69] have long hair, or behave eccentrically. This is what we expect from people who want to be taken for philosophers, but studying philosophy does not require such things. Real philosophers need only contemplate what it is to do the right thing.

---

[69] A *chiton* is like an elongated t-shirt.

17. By Musonius, from the lecture about what is the best thing to have on hand during old age[70]

(1) Another time, when an old man asked what would be the best thing to have on hand during old age, Musonius said, the very same thing that is best to have during one's youth: living the right way and in accordance with nature. To best understand what this involves, it helps to understand the nature of human beings. We did not come into existence for pleasure. Nor did horses, dogs, or cows, all of which are inferior to human beings, come into existence for pleasure. We would not consider that a horse reaches its potential by merely eating, drinking, mating without restraint, and doing none of the things which are suitable for a horse. Nor would a dog reach its potential if it indulged in all sorts of pleasure like the horse and did none of the things for which dogs are thought to be good. Nor would any other creature that, though glutted with pleasures, fails to function in a manner appropriate to it. Thus, nothing could be said to be living according to nature except the thing that demonstrates its virtue through the actions which it performs in accordance with its own nature. The nature of each creature determines, after all, the virtue characteristic of it.

(2) And so it is a reasonable assumption that a human being also does not live according to nature when he lives for pleasure, but rather when he lives for virtue. That is when he deserves praise and can rightly think well of himself and be hopeful and courageous. A cheerful disposition and secure joy automatically accompany these attributes. Indeed, the human being, alone of the creatures on earth, is the image of the divine and has the same virtues as the divine. Even when considering the gods, we are unable to think of characteristics better than intelligence and justice, or than courage and self-control. Therefore, a god, because he possesses these virtues, is not overcome by pleasure or greed; he is stronger than desire, envy, and jealousy; he is magnanimous and both a benefactor to and a lover of humanity. We believe that a god has these attributes; therefore, a human being, inasmuch as he is a copy of a god, must be considered to be like a god when he acts in accordance with nature. It is then that a human being should be envied. And because he is envied, he should be blessed as well, for none but the blessed do we envy.

---

[70] Stobaeus 4.50c.94. Chapter 50: about old age. Part c: that old age is not burdensome, and intelligence makes it worthy of much respect.

(3) And indeed it is possible for a human being to be blessed. When we come across such people—the sort of people I usually called holy and god-like—we needn't attribute their virtuous behavior to something other than human nature. Suppose someone had taken the trouble to get a proper education when still young. Suppose he had learned well the appropriate lessons and had practiced the things that require practice. In his old age, this person would use these lessons to live according to nature. He would endure without regret being deprived of the pleasures connected with youth. He would not complain about the increasing weakness of his body. He would not be upset when his neighbors overlook him or his relatives and friends neglect him. He would, after all, have an effective antidote against all these things in his own intelligence and in the education he possesses.

(4) Suppose, though, someone had not received a proper education. Suppose he sought better things and could be persuaded by proper teaching. This person would benefit if he sought to listen to advice from those who have made it their concern to know what harms and benefits us, as well as how to escape the harmful and acquire the beneficial, and how to calmly accept the things that happen which are not really bad but which seem to be. If he heard these things and was persuaded by them—since hearing without being persuaded is most unprofitable—he would deal with old age quite well in most respects. In particular, he would be set free from the fear of death—the fear that most disturbs and weighs upon old people, who seem to have forgotten the fact that death is every mortal's lot. Indeed, what makes life most wretched for old people is this very thing—the fear of death. Even the orator Isocrates believed this: it is said that, when asked how he was doing, Isocrates said as well as one could expect for a man of ninety years, but that he considered death to be the worst of evils. Someone who had learned and understood what things are truly good and what things are truly evil would not consider the thing that necessarily follows life—even the best life—to be evil.

(5) Surely the life of a good man is the best life, and death is also its end. Therefore, as I have said, if one should learn in one's old age to accept death fearlessly and boldly, one would have taken an important step towards living without regret and according to nature. He would acquire this acceptance by associating with those who are philosophers not only in name but in actuality, as long as he is willing to be persuaded by them. So I say that the best thing to have on hand during old age is what I said it was when I began this lecture: living according to nature, and doing and thinking what is appropriate. An

old man who possessed these characteristics would be most hearty and praiseworthy, and he would live happily and honorably. Anyone who thinks, to the contrary, that wealth is the greatest consolation for old people and that those who have it live without regret is mistaken. Wealth lets people enjoy food, drink, sex, and other pleasures, but wealth would never bring contentment to a wealthy person nor banish his grief. Consider, after all, how many rich men grieve, are disheartened, and think themselves wretched. Therefore wealth could not be a good defense against old age.

18. By Musonius, from the lecture about food

Part A[71]

(1) He often talked in a very forceful manner about food, on the grounds that food was not an insignificant topic and that what one eats has significant consequences. In particular, he thought that mastering one's appetites for food and drink was the beginning of and basis for self-control. On one occasion, he dispensed with his other customary topics and had the following to say about food:

(2) Just as one should choose inexpensive food over expensive food, and food that is easy to obtain over food that is hard to obtain, one should choose food suitable for a human being over food that isn't. And what is suitable for us is food from things which the earth produces: the various grains and other plants can nourish a human being quite well. Also nourishing is food from domestic animals which we don't slaughter. The most suitable of these foods, though, are the ones we can eat without cooking: fruits in season, certain vegetables, milk, cheese, and honeycombs. These foods also are easiest to obtain. Even those foods that require cooking, including grains and some vegetables, are not unsuitable; all are proper food for a human being.

(3) He argued that a meat-based diet was too crude for humans and more suitable for wild beasts. He said that it was too heavy and that it impeded mental activity. The fumes which come from it, he said, are too smoky and darken the soul. For this reason, those who eat lots of meat seem slow-witted. Since of all creatures on earth, the human being is the most closely related to the gods, he must be nourished like the gods. The vapors coming from earth and water are enough for them: what we must do, he said, is get food like that—the lightest and most pure food. If we do this, our soul would be both pure and dry, and being such, it would be best and wisest—so Heraclitus thought when he said, "A dry beam of light is the wisest and best soul."[72]

---

[71] Stobaeus 3.17.42. Chapter 17: on self-mastery.

[72] Scholars believe that this version of Heraclitus' statement is an ancient corruption of "The dry soul is the wisest and best." See John Burnet, *Early Greek Philosophy* (Cleveland: World Publishing Company, 5th printing, 1961, based on the 4th edition, Macmillan Company, 1930; the 1st edition was 1892) p. 138, nos. 74–76, n. 2.

(4) He added that when it comes to our food, we are worse than brute animals. Although they are pulled by violent desire to their food as if driven by a whip, they at least do not go to extremes and fuss about it: they are satisfied with what falls to their lot and they seek fullness only, nothing more. We humans, however, think up all sorts of devices and tricks to embellish the presentation of our food and to better amuse our palate. We have become so greedy and particular about our cuisine that, just as there are books on music and medicine, people have written books about cooking—books which will greatly increase our gastronomic pleasure, even as they ruin our health.

(5) At any rate, it is clear that those who eat too much rich food harm their bodies. Indeed, some of them resemble pregnant women who crave strange foods. Like pregnant women, they cannot tolerate ordinary food; they have ruined their digestive system. Just as inferior iron constantly needs sharpening, these people's appetites must constantly be sharpened by unmixed wine, vinegar, or some tart sauce. Compare this to the Spartan who said, "I could eat both a vulture and a buzzard," when he saw a picky eater, who had been served a tender, plump, and expensive bird, refuse to eat it because, he said, he had no appetite.

(6) Likewise, Zeno of Citium, when he was ill, did not request that dainty food be brought to him. Indeed, when the attending doctor ordered him to eat a young dove, he refused, saying, "Treat me as you would Manes." He wanted, I think, to have the same treatment that one of his slaves would have if he was ill. If slaves can get better without being fed delicacies, so can the rest of us. A good man won't expect to be coddled, any more than a slave does. Therefore, Zeno thought it best to avoid gourmet food, and he was adamant about this. He thought that someone who once experiences gourmet cuisine would want it all the time, inasmuch as the pleasure associated with drinking and eating creates in us a desire for more food and drink. We thought that this lecture about food was rather unlike the lectures Musonius customarily gave.

Part B[73]

(1) Most shameful, he said, are gluttony and a craving for gourmet food, a claim no one will deny. I have encountered very few people

---

[73] Stobaeus 3.18.37. Chapter 18: on lack of self-control.

who take steps to avoid these failings; I encounter many who long for gourmet food when it is absent and cannot control themselves when it is present—who, indeed, so glut themselves with these foods that they ruin their health. Gluttony is nothing other than lack of self-control with respect to food, and human beings prefer food that is pleasant to food that is nutritious.

(2) Furthermore, a craving for gourmet foods is nothing other than lack of moderation with respect to exotic food. Lack of moderation is always an evil thing, but its pernicious nature is best demonstrated in those who lack it in the way they greedily gulp their food. In their inability to keep their hands and eyes off food, they resemble pigs or dogs more than humans. Truly, they are deranged by their craving for gourmet foods. Their behavior towards food is very shameful; this is proved by the fact that we compare them to brute animals rather than to intelligent human beings.

(3) Since this behavior is very shameful, the opposite behavior—eating in an orderly and moderate way, and thereby demonstrating self-control—would be very good. Doing this, though, is not easy; it demands much care and training. Why? Because, although there are many pleasures which persuade human beings to do wrong and compel them to act against their own interests, the pleasure connected with food is undoubtedly the most difficult of all pleasures to combat. We encounter the other sources of pleasure less often, and we can therefore refrain from indulging in some of them for months or even years. But we will necessarily be tempted by gastronomic pleasures daily or even twice daily, inasmuch as it is impossible for a human being to live without eating.

(4) Consequently, the more often we are tempted by gastronomic pleasure, the greater the danger it presents. And, indeed, at each meal, there is not one chance for making a mistake, but several. The person who eats more than he should makes a mistake. So does the person who eats in a hurry, the person who is enthralled by gourmet food, the person who favors sweets over nutritious foods, and the person who does not share his food equally with his fellow-diners. We make another mistake in connection with food when we leave what we are supposed to be doing in order to eat, even though it isn't mealtime.

(5) Since these and other mistakes are connected with food, the person who wishes to be self-controlled must free himself of all of them and be subject to none. One way to become accustomed to this

is to practice choosing food not for pleasure but for nourishment, not to please his palate but to strengthen his body. The throat was created as a passageway for food, not as an organ for pleasure. Likewise, the human being has a stomach for the same reason that every plant has a root. Just as the root nourishes a plant by taking up nutrients from the soil, so the stomach nourishes a living creature by extracting nutrients from the food and drink it consumes. Plants take nourishment for the sake of their survival rather than for pleasure, and for humans as well, food is the medicine of life. Therefore, the goal of our eating should be staying alive rather than having pleasure—at least if we wish to follow the sound advice of Socrates, who said that many men live to eat, but that he ate to live. No right-thinking person will want to follow the masses and live to eat, as they do, in constant pursuit of gastronomic pleasures.

(6) For more evidence that the god who made humankind provided us with food and drink to keep us alive rather than give us pleasure, consider this. When the food we eat is serving its purpose—when we are digesting it and are thereby nourished and strengthened by it—our food gives us no pleasure. And yet, the time we spend digesting our food far exceeds the time we spend consuming it. If the god had wanted us to eat for pleasure, the time we spend consuming our food—and enjoying it—would have been longer.

(7) Nevertheless, to obtain those few moments of gastronomic pleasure, countless expensive foods must be prepared and brought overseas from distant lands. Cooks are more highly valued than farmers. Some people spend all their possessions to have their banquets prepared, but they are not made stronger by eating these expensive foods. Indeed, those who eat the least expensive foods are strongest. Thus, slaves are generally stronger than their masters, country folk are stronger than city folk, and the poor are stronger than the rich. Furthermore, those who eat inexpensive food can work harder, are less fatigued by working, and are sick less often than those who eat expensive food. Also, they are better able to tolerate cold, heat, lack of sleep, and so forth.

(8) But even if expensive and inexpensive food were equally effective at strengthening the body, one should choose inexpensive food, inasmuch as it is the kind of food a self-controlled person would choose and is therefore more suitable for a good man. When it comes to food, responsible people favor what is easy to obtain over what is

difficult, what involves no trouble over what does, and what is available over what isn't. To summarize the whole subject of food, I say that the goal of eating is to bring about both health and strength. Consequently, one should eat only inexpensive foods and should be concerned with decency and appropriate moderation and, most of all, with restrained and studious behavior.

19. By Musonius, from the lecture about protection from the elements[74]

(1) Having talked about food, he went on to talk about protection from the elements. One should seek protection for the body, he thought, that is modest, not expensive and excessive. One should use clothing and footwear in the same way as one uses armor: to defend the body, not to show off. The strongest weapons and those most able to keep their user safe are the best, not those that attract attention because of their sheen. Likewise, the clothing and footwear that provide the most protection for the body, not those that can attract the gaze of foolish people, are best. What is being used to provide protection must make the thing that is being protected better than itself and stronger, not weaker and worse.

(2) Those who dress to keep their skin smooth and soft, though, harm themselves, inasmuch as an enervated and soft body is inferior to one that is tough and work-hardened. Only those who dress to strengthen and build up the parts of the body they protect benefit themselves. It is a mistake to bundle up the body in a lot of clothes or envelope it in shawls or wrap up hands and feet in felt or heavy cloth—unless, that is, one is ill. It is a mistake for people to dress so that they never experience cold and heat. To the contrary, they should be somewhat cold in winter, get out in the sun in summer, and stay in the shade very little.

(3) Along these lines, one should choose to wear one *chiton* rather than two—or wear just a *himation* and no *chiton*.[75] And, if possible, it is better to go shoeless than to wear shoes: wearing shoes is rather like being shackled; shoelessness allows the feet, once they get used to it, to move freely and with agility. This is why couriers do not wear sandals on the roads. Also, competitive runners would not run fast enough if they had to run in sandals.

(4) Since we build houses to protect ourselves from the elements, these houses, too, I think should be built to provide only what is needed: to keep out cold and excessive heat, and to protect those who need to be protected from the wind. Our dwelling, in other words, should provide us the protection we could expect from a cave—one big enough for both ourselves and our stores of food.

---

[74] Stobaeus 3.1.209. Chapter 1: about virtue.

[75] For *chiton* see n. 69 above; a *himation* is a cloak.

(5) Why are there courtyards surrounded by colonnades? Why are there paints of different colors? Why are there gilded ceilings? Why the great outlays for stones, some used to pave the earth, some laid into walls, and some brought from very far away at very great expense? Aren't all these things excessive and unnecessary? One can, after all, not only live but flourish without them. Doesn't acquiring them involve both a lot of trouble and the expenditure of a lot of money—money, one should add, that could be used to help many people both publicly and privately?

(6) But isn't it more praiseworthy to help a lot of people than to live expensively? Isn't spending money on people much more noble than spending it on wood and stones? Isn't it much more worthwhile to have a lot of friends (as a result of doing good deeds cheerfully) than to have a big house? What benefits from having a big and beautiful house could match those that could be derived from using one's possessions to help one's city and its citizens?

20. By Musonius, from the lecture about furnishing a house[76]

(1) The topic of excessive expenditure for houses is connected to the topic of furnishing houses with things which are entirely unnecessary and truly extravagant. These include beds of ivory and silver or even, by Zeus, gold; tables of similar material; textiles of genuine purple and other hard-to-get dyes; and cups made of gold and silver. They also include cups made of marble or a marble-like material; these cups can be as expensive as those made of silver and gold.

(2) People crave all of these things, even though a cot provides us no worse a place to lie down on than a gold or ivory bed, and even though a cheap cloak covers a bed as well as a purple or crimson spread. We can eat as comfortably from a wooden table as from a silver one. And, by Zeus, drinking from ceramic cups can quench thirst just as well as drinking from golden ones. Indeed, wine poured into ceramic cups does not develop an off-taste and therefore has a sweeter fragrance than wine drunk from gold or silver ones.

(3) On the whole, we can judge whether various household furnishings are good or bad by determining what it takes to acquire them, use them, and keep them safe. Things that are difficult to acquire, hard to use, or difficult to guard are inferior; things that are easy to acquire, are a pleasure to use, and are easily guarded are superior. Therefore, vessels made of ceramic, cast iron, and so forth, are much better than those made of silver and gold: acquiring them is much more convenient because they are less expensive, they are more useful because—unlike vessels made of gold and silver—we can safely put them on the fire, and there is less need to safeguard them, since inexpensive things are less subject to theft than expensive ones. Furthermore, part of keeping household furnishings safe is maintaining them, and cleaning expensive items is more troublesome than cleaning inexpensive ones. An inexpensive horse that can do many useful things is better than an expensive horse that can do few. Similarly, household furnishings that are inexpensive and useful are better than those that are expensive but impractical.

(4) Why, then, are rare and expensive furnishings sought rather than those that are readily available and inexpensive? Because the good and noble things are misunderstood, and instead of pursuing things that really are good and noble, thoughtless people pursue things that

---

[76] Stobaeus 4.28.20. Chapter 28: household management.

only seem to be good, just as insane people confuse black things with white. Thoughtlessness is very close to insanity.

(5) Consider the greatest of the law-givers. Lycurgus, one of the foremost among them, drove extravagance out of Sparta and introduced thriftiness. In order to make Spartans brave, he promoted scarcity rather than excess in their lifestyle. He rejected luxurious living as a scourge and promoted a willingness to endure pain as a blessing. That Lycurgus was right is shown by the toughness of the young Spartan boys who were trained to endure hunger, thirst, cold, beatings, and other hardships. Raised in a strict environment,[77] the ancient Spartans were thought to be and in fact were the best of the Greeks, and they made their very poverty more enviable than the king of Persia's wealth.

(6) I myself would therefore choose to be sick rather than to live in luxury. Being sick harms the body only; living in luxury harms both soul and body, by making the body weak and powerless and the soul undisciplined and cowardly. Surely luxurious living fosters injustice because it also fosters greed. A person who lives extravagantly cannot help but spend a lot and therefore cannot want to spend little. Furthermore, because he wants many things, he can't refrain from trying to acquire them, and when he sets out to acquire them, he can't help grabbing for too much and being unjust. No one can acquire many things without being unjust.

(7) The person who lives luxuriously would also be entirely unjust, inasmuch as he would shrink from performing tasks he ought to undertake on behalf of his own city, if performing them meant abandoning his luxurious lifestyle. And if it was necessary to suffer hardship on behalf of friends or relatives, he would not do it, for his luxurious lifestyle would not allow him. Indeed, by the gods, someone who wants to give the gods their due must occasionally undergo hardship in order to perform sacrifices, rituals, or some other service for the gods. Someone with a luxurious lifestyle, however, will fall short on this account. He would as a result be unjust in every way—towards his city, his friends, and the gods—in his failure to do his duty. Because it is responsible for injustice, luxurious living must be completely avoided.

---

[77] There is a gap in the text here.

21. By Musonius, from the lecture about cutting hair[78]

(1) He said a man should cut his hair the way we prune vines, by removing only what is useless.[79] The beard should not be shaved, since it is a protection provided to us by nature. Furthermore, the beard is the emblem of manhood—the human equivalent of the cock's crest and the lion's mane. Therefore, a man ought to remove hair that is bothersome, but not his beard. A beard, after all, causes no bother, as long as the body is healthy and not diseased in a way that would require shaving it.

(2) Zeno, he said, was right: just as our hair grows in accordance with nature, so we should cut it in accordance with nature—when, for example, it gets too heavy or hinders our movements. Nature clearly favors too much over too little, both in plants and animals, because it is much easier and less troublesome to remove excess than to supply what is lacking. Humans should use reason to assist nature to supply what is missing and remove what is excessive.

(3) Therefore, hair should be cut to remove the excess, not to become elegant, as some think they must do. These men shave in order to look like beardless boys or, by Zeus, like boys who are just getting their beards; they also do not have their hair cut a uniform length. Yet these attempts at beautification fail and are in no way different from the primping of women who braid and style their hair in order to look more beautiful.

(4) Men who cut their hair clearly do so in order to look beautiful to those whom they wish to please. They trim and arrange their hair to attract the attention of women and boys whose praise they seek. Other men cut their hair because it bothers them, and they shave their beards. Clearly, such men have been broken by luxurious living and have become completely emasculated: they don't mind looking androgynous and womanlike, something real men would never tolerate. By Zeus, hair is no more a burden for men than feathers are for birds.

---

[78] Stobaeus 3.6.24. Chapter 6: on self-indulgence.

[79] There is a gap in the text here.

Part Two

The Sayings of Musonius

SAYINGS 22–35 COME FROM STOBAEUS: HE USES THE HEADING "BY MUSONIUS" FOR 22–28, 30–31, AND 34–35; HE USES THE HEADING "FROM THE SAME SOURCE" FOR 29 AND 32–33.

22. It is not possible to live well today unless you treat it as your last day. [Stobaeus 3.1.48 = 3.1.77. Chapter 1: about virtue.]

23. Why do we criticize tyrants, when in fact we are much worse than they are? We have the same inclinations as they do; we just lack opportunities to act on them. [Stobaeus 3.2.31. Chapter 2: about evil.]

24. If pleasure is how we should measure how attractive things are, then nothing should attract us more than self-control; and if pain is how we should measure what we should avoid, then nothing should be more painful than a lack of self-control. [Stobaeus 3.5.21. Chapter 5: about self-control.]

25. Musonius used to say that it was the height of shamelessness to think about how weak our bodies are when enduring pain, but to forget how weak they are when experiencing pleasure. [Stobaeus 3.6.21. Chapter 6: on self-indulgence.]

26. Speak of shameful things, and you will lose your reluctance to do them. [Stobaeus 3.6.22.]

27. If you work hard to do what is right, do not be upset by roadblocks; think about how many of the things in your life haven't turned out as you wanted them to, but as they should have. [Stobaeus 3.7.22. Chapter 7: on courage.]

28. Choose to die well while you can; wait too long, and it might become impossible to do so. [Stobaeus 3.7.23.]

29. It is not proper for one to die who is helpful to many while he is alive, unless by dying he is helpful to more. [Stobaeus 3.7.24.]

30. You will deserve respect from everyone if you will start by respecting yourself. [Stobaeus 3.31.6. Chapter 31: on respect.]

31. Kings soon perish who make a habit of justifying their actions to their subjects by saying "I have the power" rather than "It is my duty." [Stobaeus 4.7.14. Chapter 7: advice about kingship.]

32. Don't expect to tell others what they should do when they know that you do what you shouldn't. [Stobaeus 4.7.15.]

33. A king should want to inspire awe rather than fear in his subjects. Majesty is characteristic of the king who inspires awe, cruelty of the one who inspires fear. [Stobaeus 4.7.16.]

34. The treasures of Croesus and Cinyras we shall consider equivalent to extreme poverty. Indeed, we will hold that one man and one man only is truly wealthy—he who learns to want nothing in every circumstance. [Stobaeus 4.31d.119. Chapter 31: on wealth. Part d: that money acquired in moderation and with justice does no harm and that wealth is part of middling things.]

35. Given that all must die, it is better to die with distinction than to live long. [Stobaeus 4.51.25. Chapter 51: on death.]

::: ::: :::

SAYINGS 36 AND 37 COME FROM PLUTARCH'S *MORALIA*.

36. Sulla, this is one of Musonius' beautiful and memorable insights— that in order to protect ourselves we must live like doctors and be continually treating ourselves with reason. One must not, after using reason to treat illness of the soul, discard it, the way we discard hellebore after using it to treat illness of the body. We must instead allow reason to remain in the soul, where it will collect and guard decisions requiring good judgment. The power of reason should be compared to nutritious food rather than to drugs, since along with health it produces good behavior in those who practice it. But words of advice and warning administered when a person's emotions are at their height and boiling over accomplish little or nothing. They are like the smelling-salts given to epileptics who fall down: they revive them but do not cure the disease. [Plutarch, *Moralia* 453 D–E (Loeb VI, W. C. Helmbold): "On Controlling Anger." The speakers in this dialogue are Sextius Sulla, Plutarch's friend, and C. Minicius Fundanus, a friend of Pliny the Younger. Fundanus is speaking to Sulla about Musonius.]

37. Rutilius,[80] that well-known man in Rome, came up to Musonius and said, "Musonius, Zeus the savior, whom you pattern yourself after and try to be like, does not borrow money." Musonius smiled and said, "He does not *lend* it either." (Rutilius, in the act of lending money to Musonius, was chiding him for borrowing it.) [Plutarch, *Moralia* 830B (Loeb X, H. N. Fowler): "On the necessity of not borrowing."]

::: ::: :::

SAYINGS 38–42 COME FROM STOBAEUS WHO HEADS ALL BUT 41 "BY RUFUS [MUSONIUS] FROM EPICTETUS' REMARKS [OR FROM EPICTETUS] ON FRIENDSHIP"; 41 IS HEADED "FROM THE SAME SOURCE."

38. Of the things that exist, Zeus has put some in our control and some not in our control. In our control is the most beautiful and important thing, the thing because of which even the god himself is happy—namely, the proper use of our impressions. Such use brings freedom, prosperity, serenity, and stability; it also brings justice, law, self-control, and complete virtue. All other things he did not put in our control. Therefore, we must agree with the god: after we have divided matters in this way, we must concern ourselves absolutely with the things that are under our control and entrust the things not in our control to the universe. And whether it be our children, our fatherland, our body, or anything else that the universe demands, we must yield them readily. [Epictetus, Fragment 4 = Stobaeus 2.8.30. Chapter 8: about things in our control.]

39. Who among us is not amazed at the action of Lycurgus the Spartan? When a young man who had injured Lycurgus' eye was sent by the people to be punished in whatever way Lycurgus wanted, he did not punish him. He instead both educated him and made him a good man, after which he led him to the theater. While the Spartans looked on in amazement, he said: "This person I received from you as an unruly and violent individual. I give him back to you as a good man and proper citizen." [Epictetus, Fragment 5 = Stobaeus 3.19.13. Chapter 19: about putting up with evil.]

---

[80] Publius Rutilius Lupus was a grammarian of the first century AD who is cited in Quintilian 9.3 *passim* in a discussion of figures of speech. The verbal play between Musonius and Rutilius depends on the same verb which means "lend" in the active and "borrow" in the middle.

40. But more than anything, it is the function of nature to make our choice for action harmonize with the correct perception of the appropriate and beneficial. [Epictetus, Fragment 6 = Stobaeus 3.20.60. Chapter 20: on anger.]

41. Believing that we will be scorned by others unless we destroy every enemy we meet is characteristic of extremely ignoble and mindless men. We say that a contemptible person is marked by his inability to harm others, but such a person is much more marked by his inability to help them. [Epictetus, Fragment 7 = Stobaeus 3.20.61. Chapter 20: on anger.]

42. Such was and is and will be the nature of the universe. It is not possible for things that come into being to come into being differently than they do now. Human beings and the other animals on the earth are involved in the turning and changing of the universe, as are divine beings. By Zeus, the four elements themselves change and are transformed: earth becomes water, which becomes air, which in turn becomes aether, at which point the process of change is reversed. If one tries to focus his attention on these things and convinces himself to accept willingly things that must happen, he will live a moderate and harmonious life. [Epictetus, Fragment 8 = Stobaeus 4.44.60. Chapter 44: that those who are human beings must bear whatever happens with nobility and that they are obligated to live virtuously.]

⁝⁝⁝ ⁝⁝⁝ ⁝⁝⁝

SAYINGS 43–48 COME FROM ARRIAN'S *DISCOURSES* OF EPICTETUS.

43. Thrasea used to say: "I would rather be killed today than be exiled tomorrow." What then did Rufus say to him? "If you choose that as the heavier thing, what a foolish choice! If you choose it as the lighter, who has given you that choice? Are you not willing to learn to be satisfied with what you have been given?" [Epictetus, *Discourses* 1.1.26.]

44. (30) [Musonius:] "Why are we still so lazy, easy-going, and slothful? Why do we look for excuses that will let us avoid the work and lost sleep attendant to the study of philosophy?" (31) [Epictetus:] "If I made a mistake in these arguments, I didn't thereby kill my father, did I?" [Musonius:] "Slave, how was your father involved in this in order for you to kill him? What did you do? There was only one mistake to make in this argument, and you made it." (32) I myself made the remark quoted above to Rufus when he upbraided me for failing to discover the part that had been left out of a syllogism. I also said: "It's not as if I burned down the Capitol," to which he replied, "Slave, what is left out here *is* the Capitol." (33) Are "burning the Capitol" and "killing one's father" the only mistakes one can make? Are we not making mistakes if we use impressions at random, in vain, and by chance; if we do not pay attention to reason, proof, or even a quibble; in a word, if we do not carefully analyze what is to our advantage and what is not? [Epictetus, *Discourses* 1.7.30–33.]

45. (29) [Epictetus is speaking:] To test me, Rufus used to make comments like this: "Your master will do such and such a thing to you." (30) When I answered him that this was the human condition, he said: "Then why should I ask him for what I can get from you?" (31) For it is pointless and foolish to get from another what one gets from oneself. (32) Since I can get a great soul and a noble character from myself, am I to get a farm, money, or some office from you? Absolutely not. [Epictetus, *Discourses* 1.9.29–32.]

46. (9) Persuading lazy young men is as hard as catching cheese with a fish-hook. Intelligent young men are even more devoted to philosophy if you turn them away. (10) Therefore, Rufus often turned would-be students away in order to assess their intelligence. He used to say: "A stone, because of its makeup, will return to earth if you throw it up in the air. Likewise, the more one pushes the intelligent person away from the life he was born for, the more he inclines towards it." [Epictetus, *Discourses* 3.6.9–10.]

47. When Galba was assassinated, someone asked Rufus: "Is the world ruled by providence now?" Rufus replied: "Did I ever, even in an offhand way, use Galba as an example to show that the world is ruled by providence?" [Epictetus, *Discourses* 3.15.14.]

48. (29) [Epictetus is speaking:] Rufus used to say: "If you have time enough to praise me, then I know that what I am saying is worthless." And after saying this, he went on to say things that caused each of us who sat there to think that someone at some time had given him revealing information about us: he grasped our circumstances so well, and he placed our faults before our eyes so effectively. (30) Students, the philosopher's school is a doctor's office. You must leave not pleased, but pained. You do not come in healthy: one of you has hurt his shoulder, another has an abscess, another a fistula, another a headache. (31) Am I to sit you down and tell you clever slogans and sayings so that you praise me as you leave, even though the shoulder is no better than it was, the head still hurts, and the abscess and fistula remain? (32) Do young men leave home for these reasons and leave behind their parents, friends, kinfolk, and small property so that they may yell "hooray" when you utter witticisms? Did Socrates do this, or Zeno, or Cleanthes? [Epictetus, *Discourses* 3.23.29–32.]

::: ::: :::

Sayings 49–52 come from Aulus Gellius, *Attic Nights,* and are in Latin, although Gellius intersperses some Greek.

49. (1) The story goes that Musonius the philosopher used to say this about praise: "Suppose that a philosopher urges, warns, persuades, rebukes, or expands upon some theme or other of his doctrines, and his listeners babble commonplace, ordinary words of praise off the top of their mindless heads. Suppose, too, that they shout or gesture because they are moved, swayed, and delighted by the loveliness of his expressions, and by the rhythms of his words—by certain trills, as it were, of his oration. Then you can be certain that the speaker is wasting his breath and the listeners are not learning anything. They are not hearing a philosopher speak; they are instead listening to a flutist play."

(2) He said also: "The mind of someone listening to a philosopher, so long as what is said is useful and wholesome and so long as it conveys remedies for errors and vices, is too engrossed to have time for wild and extravagant praise.

(3) Any listener who isn't completely decadent ought to shudder during a philosopher's discourse and be shamed into silence. He ought, by turns, to repent, rejoice, be amazed, (4) and show differing expressions and changing feelings to go along with how the philosopher's presentation has affected him and his understanding of the part of his mind which is healthy and the part which is sick."

(5) He also used to say that admiration can give rise to great praise, but that the greatest admiration gives rise not to words, but to silence.

(6) "Therefore," he said, "the wisest of poets, in his *Odyssey*, has the people listening to Ulysses, as he finished giving the very brilliant account of his labors, respond not by jumping up, shouting, and making lots of noise, but by falling silent as if stupefied and struck dumb by words which delighted their ears and arrested their power of speech:

> Thus he spoke, and they all stayed softly in silence,
> and they were held by a magic spell in the shadowy hall."[81]

[Gellius 5.1: That the philosopher Musonius criticized and condemned a philosopher's being praised by those who shout and gesture in their praise as he is giving a discourse.]

50. Herodes said: "Musonius ordered a thousand sesterces to be given to a charlatan who was portraying himself as a philosopher. When several people said that this good-for-nothing was a bad and devious man, worthy of nothing good, Musonius smiled and said: 'Then money is what he deserves.'" [Gellius 9.2.8: In what words Herodes Atticus reproached a fellow who assumed the name and manner of a philosopher by means of false clothing and get-up.]

51. (1) When we were still young students, we were told the following Greek aphorism, attributed to the philosopher Musonius. Since it was truly and brilliantly stated and expressed with a few polished words, we gladly memorized it:

(2) "If you accomplish something good with hard work, the labor passes quickly, but the good endures; if you do something shameful in pursuit of pleasure, the pleasure passes quickly, but the shame endures."

(3) Later we read that very same aphorism in a speech of Cato which he delivered to the knights at Numantia. Although Cato's version was wordier and less elegantly stated than Musonius' Greek aphorism, Cato's version comes first and is thus more ancient and must therefore be considered more venerable.

(4) Here is what Cato said: "Consider this. If you have accomplished something good through hard work, that labor will quickly disappear. If something is done well by you, it will not disappear as long as you live. But if you have done something wicked in the pursuit of

---

[81] Homer, *Odyssey*, 13.1–2.

pleasure, the pleasure will quickly disappear, but the wicked thing will stay with you forever." [Gellius 16.1: Greek words of the philosopher Musonius which are worthy and useful to be heard and followed. An opinion of equal worth was said by Marcus Cato many years before to Roman knights at Numantia.]

52. We were spending the Saturnalia at Athens quite pleasantly and modestly. We did not, however, let our minds go lax—for, Musonius says, "to let one's mind go lax is, in effect, to lose it"—but we did take it easy and loosen them up a little with the pleasant and honest delights of conversation. [Gellius 18.2.1: The sorts of questions we used to discuss during the Saturnalia at Athens.]

::: ::: :::

SAYING 53 COMES FROM AELIUS ARISTIDES, *ORATIONS* LII.

53. Someone once tried to encourage me by quoting a saying of Musonius: "Musonius," he said, "when he wanted to encourage someone who was tired and who had given up, upbraided him and said: 'Why do you stand there? What are you looking for? Do you expect the god himself to come and speak to you? Cut out the dead part of your soul, and you will recognize the god.'" According to him, this was a saying of Musonius.[82]

---

[82] In Saying 53, we have an excerpt from a speech. Aristides quotes someone who himself quotes Musonius.

Appendix I: Musonius in Philostratus

From Philostratus, *Life of Apollonius of Tyana* 4.46: An exchange of letters between Apollonius of Tyana and Musonius[83]

(1) At about that same time, Musonius happened to be held in the prisons of Nero. They say that of all people, Musonius pursued philosophy most perfectly. They (Apollonius and Musonius) did not openly talk with each other, since Musonius was reluctant to do this lest they would both be in danger. They conducted their association through letters carried by Menippus and Damis, who were regular visitors to the prison. We will omit the letters that are not about important subjects and present those that make important points.

(2) "Apollonius sends greetings to Musonius the philosopher. I want to come to you and share in your doctrine and stay with you so that I may help you in some way—or don't you believe that Heracles once set Theseus free from Hades? Write what you wish. Farewell."

(3) "Musonius sends greetings to Apollonius the philosopher. Your intentions are praiseworthy, but the man who offers a defense and demonstrates that he acted justly sets himself free. Farewell."

(4) "Apollonius sends greetings to Musonius the philosopher. Socrates the Athenian did not want to be freed by his friends, went to trial, and died. Farewell."

(5) "Musonius sends greetings to Apollonius the philosopher. Socrates died because he did not offer a defense, but I will offer one. Farewell."

Commentary:

Tim Whitmarsh cites the above exchange in his discussion of how Musonius' persona is constructed in relation to Socrates, but it is not clear if he considers the letters authentic.[84]

---

[83] There are two Loeb editions of Philostratus' *Life of Apollonius of Tyana*: F. C. Conybeare (1912) and Christopher P. Jones (2005). The above exchange is included in Hense's edition of Musonius under the heading *Epistulae Spuriae*, letters attributed to Musonius, probably pseudonymously.

[84] Whitmarsh, *Greek Literature and the Roman Empire*, p. 150 (see above, p. 18, n. 22) and also "Greece is the World: Exile and Identity in the Second Sophistic," in *Being Greek under Rome*, edited by Simon Goldhill (Cambridge, 2001), p. 283.

Musonius is mentioned several other times in Philostratus' *Life of Apollonius of Tyana*. In Book 4.35 the subject is Nero's hostility towards philosophers. (He thought they practiced divination, and emperors did not like people who tried to figure out a future without them.) This is where Musonius' imprisonment is first mentioned—although curiously, he is identified as a Babylonian. In Book 7.16 Musonius is described as having been exiled by Nero to the waterless island of Gyara, where he discovered a spring. People went there to visit him and later went there to see the spring. Here Musonius is identified as a Tyrian, but scholars agree that what was meant was *Tyrrhenian*, Greek for *Etruscan*.

Finally, in Book 5.19 we read that Demetrius the philosopher "said that he had encountered Musonius at the Isthmus of Corinth.[85] Musonius was in chains, having been ordered to help dig a canal across the isthmus. Demetrius offered the usual greetings. Musonius took hold of his mattock and struck at the ground vigorously. He then lifted up his head, and said, 'Do I upset you, Demetrius, to be digging the isthmus for Greece? I wonder what you would have thought if you saw me playing the cithara like Nero?' I will omit the many other striking things Musonius said, since I don't want to misrepresent the off-handed way he said them."

---

[85] This incident inspired a short dialogue transmitted with Lucian's work called "Nero or the Digging of the Isthmus": see vol. 8 of the Loeb edition of Lucian, edited by M. D. MacLeod (1967). This dialogue is thought to be by one of the Philostrati (there are several), probably by the author of the *Life of Apollonius*. Tim Whitmarsh studies this text in detail: "Greek and Roman in Dialogue: The Pseudo-Lucianic Nero," *Journal of Hellenic Studies* 119 (1999) 142–60. The Philostrati are late second–early third century AD. Lucian was born about AD 120.

Appendix II: Letter to Pankratides

Much less well-known than the exchange of letters between Apollonius and Musonius is a long letter attributed to Musonius which purports to explain to someone named Pankratides how the study of philosophy will benefit him and his sons. It is found in a manuscript which belonged to Cardinal Mazarin and was included in a collection of Greek letter writers published by Rudolph Hercher in 1871.[86] Hercher provided a Latin translation, but the letter has not until now been translated into any other language. In his edition of Musonius, Hense printed Hercher's Greek text with a critical apparatus which I have consulted as well.[87] This kind of pseudonymous letter was a very popular writing exercise in the period of the Second Sophistic.[88]

(1) From what we have been told about you and from what you have written to your sons, I have concluded that you understand philosophy correctly and do not view it in the same way as ordinary people do. I am eager to rejoice with you about your sons and to pray that in the future they do not fall away into some other pursuit but keep to their present purpose and pursue philosophy to its goal, in which case they might turn out well and be able to repay the benefits they have received from you. Indeed, generally speaking, there are two qualities which are responsible for people living in an orderly and systematic fashion: experience and self-mastery. How can we do what we must, either for ourselves or for others, if we are limited by ignorance and a lack of self-control?

(2) I am convinced that we must actively seek deliverance from these evils, inasmuch as we were created to live in an orderly and decent manner: that is why nature has given us reason as an overseer and guide. Indeed, we can't be freed from ignorance and lack of self-control without entrusting ourselves to reason's care. This remedy presents itself and continually transforms our motivations from being

---

[86] Rudolph Hercher, *Epistolographi Graeci* (Paris: Didot, 1871), pp. 401–4, 51–52. The paragraph divisions are Hercher's.

[87] Hense, "Epistulae Spuriae," pp. 137–42.

[88] Patricia A. Rosenmeyer, *Ancient Greek Literary Letters* (Routledge, 2006), pp. 97-99.

contrary to nature to being in accordance with nature. It endeavors to strike out the wicked judgments that are embedded in our soul as a result of misperception and to free us of them. It tries to introduce healthy judgments that are in accordance with nature or to repair unsound judgments.

(3) When judgments achieve strength and stability, they properly direct all aspects of our life so that we unfailingly perceive the things that concern us and make our actions conform to what is proper. Since treatment of the soul not only promises these results but provides them, who could more rightly be called on to aid your children than yourself? Don't you, their father, prefer for them to be happy? Aren't you prepared to endure anything in order to see them counted among good men? Isn't this why you had them and raised them? Didn't you continually pray on their behalf to the gods for just these things?

(4) Since you seek to live a virtuous and decent life, wouldn't you want your children to exercise restraint in eating and drinking, to control their sexual urges, and to have children only when it is appropriate? Wouldn't you want them to be satisfied with a little sleep for rest and to be dressed in simple and honest clothing, clean and covering appropriately what nature demands be covered? Wouldn't you want them to comport themselves with modesty and discretion, so that no one would dare to do or say anything indecent around them? Wouldn't you want them to be prepared to devote their whole body and every part of it for what it has been created whenever they want and need to?

(5) Wouldn't you want your sons to weigh their duties towards gods and humans and to behave towards gods with reverence and holiness and towards humans with justice and holiness? Wouldn't you want them to honor country over their parents, since this is what wise parents would want, and to honor their parents over other family members and relatives? But wouldn't you also want them to award the highest honor to [Zeus,] the father of their parents? Wouldn't you want it to seem disrespectful for you to ask or blame them for something? And wouldn't you want to feel it necessary to thankfully and mindfully repay their services, since this would allow old kindnesses to be repaid with new ones? Wouldn't you want your sons to be ready to fight on behalf of country, parents, and family, and to die for them if necessary? And if country, parents, and family are angry, wouldn't you want your children to accept calmly not just the words but also the blows and wounds that spring from anger rather than premeditation? And while doing this, wouldn't you want them to

take care not for themselves but for their parents, lest they be harmed by the experience?

(6) What would you endure to gain the assurance that they would live in one house their whole life, would make themselves and their possessions available to each other, and would spend the rest of their life amiably enjoying the same pursuits and relaxations? Wouldn't you want them to be in that situation? Wouldn't you want them to be disdainful of death, pain, and public opinion—things to which the crowd has been enslaved, the crowd which is carried and dragged along hither and yon like an ignominious slave by the power of these things? Wouldn't you pray that they attain the trait that past generations found it easy to possess but the current generation, because of the misperception involved with such things, finds it difficult to possess? If they do, they will not measure everything by money, and they will consider themselves, their parents, and their children to be worth more than mere possessions. Wouldn't you pray that they seek to acquire only what is necessary for themselves and their household and to disdain luxuries? People who pursue luxuries are driven, both in private and in public, to commit countless wicked and deadly acts.

(7) You must pray for these things. And shouldn't you also pray for your sons to be able to rule and to judge in accordance with the law and the dictates of justice, and for them to do so in concert with each other? Shouldn't you pray for them to be circumspect in their speech and to live in accordance with a philosophy founded on reason and proper values? This philosophy will prepare them to act when action is called for, and it will guide them when they fight for sacred things—for country, parents, friends, truth, laws—on behalf, that is, of those who are wronged. I do not think that you or any other wise person advocates a political philosophy that aims not at these things but at their opposites.

(8) If these things are indeed to be prayed for and sought, then since philosophy alone can bring them about, doesn't it follow that we should pursue philosophy? The person who strives to reason and act correctly is doing philosophy. The person who reasons with care thereby takes care of his country, father, brothers, and friends—in a word, everybody. Nature has made us spectators of the world and the things in it by endowing us (but not animals) with reason. She expects us to emulate the gods, who are our ultimate leaders, benefactors, and parents. She expects us to repay them with ready obedience and to accept them as caring and kindly leaders of human beings in affairs both public and private.

(9) Philosophy tells us that when we mingle the human and the divine in law and justice, we are destined by nature to gain perfection and be regulated and blessed by the same law and justice as the divine. Because our behavior will be formed by correct doctrine, we will live happily. We will also bring our life to a happy end, like the people who gracefully play a role in a well-written drama.

(10) So be confident, Pankratides: don't just allow your sons to study philosophy; encourage them to do so. Also, study it yourself and urge them on with frank discussions. Do this, and you will be able to say even to blood relatives that you raised your children with the interests not only of the family but the country in mind, inasmuch as you provided it with the most desirable sort of citizen.

(11) If you will discuss things frankly and strive to behave in a proper manner, you will collectively be pursuing philosophy. You will find yourself in a contest supervised by the gods. To prepare for this contest, you will rely on your own meager resources, but you will also rely on revered traditions—something only a serious philosopher could do. In entering this contest, you will participate in the broader contest to rid ourselves not of things that are in accordance with nature but things that cause us grief and agitation.

(12) In this contest, the unprepared person will inevitably be defeated and, once defeated, will fall into slavery and despair—a situation from which he can't excuse himself by swearing an oath. We are defeated in this contest by eternal laws, natural laws, and legislative laws, all of which order us to behave ourselves and live justly and piously. I think that you, as a father, will accept this advice from a father, and that you yourself will thereby become a better person and will join with your sons in pursuing the best. I greet you in part because of your good will towards us. Know that you are loved by me. As long as you all pursue philosophy, you will be surrounded by such friends and by others as well.

Acknowledgments

Two individuals who played important roles in the creation of this book were Tim Beck, who did copyediting, and Keith Seddon, who acted as literary midwife in seeing this book through the publication process. We would like to take this opportunity to thank them both. William King read the translation in its early stages against the Greek and also deserves our thanks.

About the Translator

Cynthia King is associate professor, emerita, of the Classics Department of Wright State University in Dayton, Ohio. For the CANE (Classical Association of New England) Short Texts in Greek and Latin Series, she did an edition of *The Tablet of Cebes* to use with the first edition of *Athenaze: An Introduction to Ancient Greek*, published by Oxford University Press. This edition of the *Tablet* was expanded and incorporated into *Workbook II* of the second edition of *Athenaze* (2004).

About the Editor

William B. Irvine is professor of philosophy at Wright State University in Dayton, Ohio. He is the author of *A Guide to the Good Life: The Ancient Art of Stoic Joy* (Oxford University Press, 2009).